BLACK TENTS OF ARABIA

BLACK TENTS
OF ARABIA

(*My Life Among the Bedouins*)

BY

CARL R. RASWAN

Hungry Mind Press
Saint Paul, Minnesota

Published by Hungry Mind Press
1648 Grand Avenue
Saint Paul, MN 55105

First Hungry Mind Press printing 1998
Printed in the United States of America

10 9 8 7 6 5 4 3 2 1

ISBN: 1-886913-21-8
LCCN: 98-70347

Cover design: Will Powers
Cover photograph: Gary Morris, courtesy www.arttoday.com
Inset photographs: Carl R. Raswan

To
my
beloved
PARENTS
for
all their
love and patience
with me during my
years as a wandering
Ishmaelite

Foreword

IN THE COURSE of my twenty-two years off and on among the Bedouins of Arabia, migrating, hunting, raiding, starving and feasting with them, I experienced wonderful friendships, and I am indebted to many of these desert friends:

To "The Lord of the land of his fathers", *the King of Arabia: 'Abd el-'Aziz ibn Sa'ûd el Wahhab* and his governors and chiefs in Nejd, Hasa, Jauf, and Kaf, and his representatives in Damascus, Cairo and London.

And to *Amir Nuri Sha'lan,* his family and the tribe of the Ruala, for the unique opportunities which enabled me to gain an intimate knowledge of Arab traditions and Bedouin customs, and to traverse so much unknown territory, so that I came to understand the soul of their mysterious country and the minds of these dwellers in the black tents of Ishmael; favours which alone made it possible to collect the material which has gone to the making of this work.

I feel a deep sense of gratitude for the inspiration kindled within me by the work and ideals of the late *Lady Anne Blunt,* which have sustained me in my quest for the true Arab horse. And to *Mr. W. K. Kellogg,* of Battle Creek, Michigan, who dedicated his ranch and stud farm in California to students of animal husbandry with an endowment large enough to secure forever the raising of pure-bred Arab horses.

To *Charles Doughty,* England's classic traveller in the "Island of the Arabs", I owe the fact that from my very first day in the wilderness I could look with a "gentle-spirit" and "tender-heart" upon the "ferocious desert" and the "fanatical hostility of the Arabs", and come out with the intense satisfaction that I had lived in peace under the goat-hair tents of the Ishmaelites.

I am also greatly indebted to *Mr. J. K. Wright* of the American Geographical Society and to *"Sheykh Musa er Rueyli" (Prof. A. Musil of Prague)* because his publications enabled me to take a new and more intelligent interest in my travels in Arabia and especially among the Ruala, into whose fellowship we both (though we never met) have been adopted as members of the chief's family and the tribe.

My debt to *"Colonel Lawrence of Arabia"* is great, in that he has been my constant companion through the pages of his book on my last eight journeys, and has fortified my soul by his incomparable example of perseverance to carry me through the most trying conditions of the desert. I have met many of his old companions and also enemies, and whether they loved or feared him, they all agree that "Aurans" was the most sincere friend that ever came from Europe to take up the Arab cause, though most of them regretted that he did not have a chance to side with Ibn Sa'ûd. I have also to express my sincere thanks to *Mr. Gomer Williams* for the valuable help he has given me in the preparation of this book.

There are many others, both in Arabia and in the Western World, to whom I owe my thanks for their kind and sympathetic helpfulness.

Contents

PART I

THE HEIRS OF ISHMAEL

I	THE YOUNG PRINCE OF THE RUALA, AMIR FUAZ	3
II	FARIS—"A FRIEND OF GOD"	12
III	THE LONE SHEPHERDESS	19
IV	I MEET MY BLOOD BROTHER AGAIN	27
V	LOVE IN THE DESERT	32
VI	THE COMMANDER OF OUR CAMEL-SADDLES	38
VII	DEATH IN THE DESERT	43
VIII	PANTHER AND OSTRICH	51
IX	THE NUFUD	57
X	SANDSTORM	63
XI	DAYS OF EASE	68
XII	CAMELS, WOMEN, CHILDREN—AND LOCUSTS	72
XIII	TUËMA	79
XIV	THE HUNGER MARCH	82
XV	FAMINE AND WAR	86
XVI	A NEW LEASE OF LIFE	94

Contents

XVII   The War Goddess 98

XVIII   The Land of Promise 101

XIX   The Ambush 119

XX   "The Cloud in My Eyes" 128

XXI   The "Ark of Ishmael" 141

PART II

HUNTING AND WARFARE

XXII   Ali, the "Protector" 147

XXIII   Adventures with the "Tin Lizzie" . . 154

XXIV   With the Tai' and Shammar Bedouins . . 160

XXV   Honour among Thieves 175

XXVI   The Stealing of the Mare 186

XXVII   Anaga—the Falcon 192

XXVIII   The Young Gazelle Buck 199

Introduction

"I took care of thee in the wilderness." HOSEA xiii, 5.

IT IS MY desire in this book to deal with things of human interest rather than with scientific questions, and where possible to allow my adventures and experiences with the men and animals of the wilderness to comprise my story.

My soul is bound up in this romantic "Arabia Deserta." The great peace and calm of the Arabian wilderness holds me in thrall—that tremendous quietude, which on the last day of the creation must have brooded over the whole world. In the desert I breathe freely and the accumulated ballast of civilized life falls away, like a great burden from my shoulders. Even now I am amazed to think how little man really needs to be happy, and how carefree one is with nothing but the merest necessities of life.

My expeditions into the desert and my life among the Arabs were not prompted by scientific aspirations; the Arab horse was the lodestone. The "white patches" on the map did not attract me so much, even though I lived for the most part in quite unknown regions never, or very rarely, visited by Europeans. It was not even the call of adventure which led my footsteps into the wilder parts of the Near East, but just the love of horses and in particular of the splendid Arab horse. So intense was (and is) my passion for this noble animal, that I wished to meet him in his native pastures and there learn his history and the secrets of his breeding; and, if there was a secondary interest, it was to enquire into the wanderings of the Bedouin tribes. This grew more fascinating the further I proceeded, so that I came to study the geographical features of their pasture-areas and lines of migration, their historic past and ethnographical peculiarities—subjects on which I have published in various lands a series of special articles, maps, and tables.[1]

The Arabian peninsula is inconceivably vast; its area is half as great as that of the United States of America. My wanderings, naturally, stretched over only a part of Arabia, the highland plateau of the Bedouins that lies inland.

Although I touched the Red Sea and the Persian Gulf more than once, I have never yet visited such well-known places as Aden or Oman, not to mention Mecca and the Rub-el-Khali, which was crossed for the first time by two Englishmen (Bertram Thomas and St. John Philby) only a few years ago. I claim one thing, however: that during my sojourn in Arabia, I lived entirely as a Bedouin. I had never any need to deny my

[1] *American Geographical Society* (New York, 1930); *Asia* (New York, 1929); *Hippologische Sammlung*, Schickhardt and Ebner (Stuttgart, 1930); *Sportologue* (Los Angeles, 1931); *Sankt Georg* (Berlin, 1930–33); *Berliner Illustrierte Zeitung* (Berlin, 1933); *Country Life* (London, 1934); *Sphere* (London, 1934); *Strand* London, 1935), etc., and Bulletins of the Agricultural Colleges and Animal Breeding Associations in Hungary, Poland, Russia, Japan, Argentina, Egypt, etc.

race or my creed amongst the Arabs. I was never once the butt of their mockery or suffered at their hands any discourtesy.

The reason that I was allowed to live with them on the most intimate terms and was implicitly trusted by them may perhaps be explained by the simple fact that I refrained from mingling in their politics, except when invited to give my opinion in internal tribal affairs. Furthermore, I was careful to adhere to all their cherished customs and prejudices, particularly those relating to their women. These are strict, and no European can hope to gain the complete confidence of a Bedouin without studied observance of them.

Like the desert itself, the Bedouins, looked upon from the outside, have a forbidding appearance; but the closer one lives to them, the better one comes to know them and is the more astonished at their placid unconcern.

The most astounding thing, which will ever command my admiration, is the equanimity with which the Bedouin leads his family and his herds from the oases and cultivated lands into the wilderness and across desert areas, which appear to be absolutely barren. The first cloud proclaiming the advent of rain lures him irresistibly to the highlands of the Hamad and the flint desert or into the sand dunes of the Nufud. After the first rains the bold camel-plunderers also leave their tents. With their war-mares tied to their racing camels, they ride out into the blue, often covering a thousand miles, "and sit on the roads (as the holy script says) and lie in wait for booty like an Arab in the desert. . . ."

In this book my object, therefore, is to tell the story of these wandering herdsmen and mounted raiders, and my experiences amongst them.

Amman,
    Transjordania.

Part One

THE HEIRS OF ISHMAEL

๑ I ๑

The Young Prince of the Ruala,
Amir Fuaz

THE SETTING SUN painted in delicate tints the naked hills of the Jabal Ruak.

In the southwest, black tents and fawn-coloured camel-herds covered the close-cropped plain of Tueyf. Armed men on nimble mares galloped towards us, as I, accompanied by a few horsemen, for the first time in my life approached the woven goat-hair "houses", a camp of the Ruala Bedouins.

The mounted sentries, who had come to meet us, conducted us to the smoke-blackened tent of an old slave. It was here I was received by Amir Nuri Sha'lan, the grey-bearded prince of the tribe.

The aged Nuri had lately (it was two years before the outbreak of the Great War) exchanged, not without reason, his own comfortable tent for the mean shelter of one of his slaves. He was in hiding. He had been warned of the activity of blood-avengers, men of his own kith and kin. For in the struggle for the headship of the tribe, he had shot one of his brothers with his own hand, and his slaves had killed another. Their sons, now grown to manhood, were not only seeking to avenge the murder of their fathers, but also to wrest the position of chieftain from Nuri Sha'lan.

While Nuri thus stood at bay against enemies in his

own tribe, his eldest son, Nauaf, was charged with leading the Ruala against their external enemies. Nuri was the father of a large family and was in fact credited with eighty-two children, of whom thirty-seven were sons, nearly all of whom died violent deaths.

A few days after this first meeting with Nuri Sha'lan, I paid a visit to Nauaf, whose tents were pitched a day's ride away, by the rain-water pools of Rukuban, one hundred and twenty odd miles east of Damascus.

Nauaf differed greatly from his father. He lacked the old *Sheykh's* strong personality. Nor had he the talent to organize for warfare a tribe so vast as the Ruala, with its seven thousand tents, thirty-five thousand souls, and over three hundred thousand camels.

He had just mustered another small camel-troop to strengthen his forces operating against Jauf, the oasis at the southeastern end of the wide, fertile depression of the Wadi Sirhan. They had already taken a few lesser fortified outposts. But these successes had brought Nauaf little credit: neither from his own tribesmen nor from the subjugated settlers could he win the respect which would have consolidated his position. Moreover, this attack on Jauf was a reversal of tribal policy. From of old the Ruala had peacefully traded with that oasis, bartering their camels, wool, cheese, and butter for dates, barley, salt, coffee, tent fittings, camel-saddles, and textiles. Suddenly, and quite against the old *Sheykh's* intentions, Nauaf conceived the scheme of monopolizing that trade for himself and occupying the oasis as a strategic stronghold from which to dominate Northern Arabia and the caravan routes to Nejd.

Within sight of Jauf opens out the great, red-sand desert of the Nufud, which extends more than three hundred miles from east to west and nearly two hundred miles from north to south. Its northern half, called El-Labbe, forms the proper grazing ground of the Ruala. Their real home is there. The southern part is held by the Shammar Bedouins, who have made Hayil, on the southern edge of the Nufud, their trading centre.

Until after the Great War, the Shammar were ruled by Ibn Rashid, a renegade governor of the Ibn Sa'ûd family, who, with his Negro bodyguard, had rebelled against his masters and had taken Hayil. Ibn Sa'ûd, however, succeeded in recovering that dominant position, which secured him undisputed power in Central Arabia (Nejd, Kasim, and Hejaz).

The efforts Ibn Sa'ûd made to weld all the tribes into one national unit, his subjugation, in campaign after campaign, of all *Shiyukhs* (*Sheykhs*) who resisted him, are well known. Now, at the time of my first sojourn in the land of the Bedouins, this Ibn Rashid, the traitor governor, had still the greater part of Inner Arabia under his power. He became so completely sovereign that his former masters, the Ibn Sa'ûd family, had to live for decades in exile, while the "Black Princes" held sway over the towns and oases as well as the many Bedouin tribes of Central Arabia. In the history of Arabia there are few bolder achievements than Ibn Sa'ûd's recovery, with a mere handful of men, of his capital, Riyadh, his subjugation of Hayil and the Shammar, until he, adding success to success, became at length the virtual dictator of Arabia, to whom the world to-day accords its sincere admiration.

At the time of which I speak, however—in 1912—Nauaf, the son of Nuri Sha'lan, was at war against the hereditary enemy of the Ruala, the Shammar Bedouins and their ruler, Ibn Rashid, who held Jauf. The capture of that oasis was the objective of long and bitter fighting. Much blood was shed; every year took its long toll of human lives. Now, however, Nauaf had come close to his goal and soon Jauf actually fell into his hands.

Nauaf had three sons, amongst whom was the young Prince, Amir Fuaz; it is with him I would begin my tale. For to this child I owe the fact that I was privileged to live with the Ruala as one of them, that I was permitted to visit them eleven times in twenty-two years; that I wandered, hunted, and fought with them; that on horseback or camel-back, I crossed and recrossed their grazing-grounds year in and year out; that I was adopted into the tribe as a Rueyli chieftain; and that they knew and loved me as I knew and loved them.

Amir Fuaz was just eight years of age. Even so, he already had the reputation of being an adroit rider and a good shot, though his legs were yet rather short to grip the flanks of a mare and his arms to weak to balance a carbine for any length of time. "Wordly learning", as the Arabs call reading and writing, held no interest for him. He preferred to go camel-riding with me or to join in the hunt. His mother, Misha'il, who had gone blind, proudly related to me that it was an omen of good for the future that Nuri Sha'lan had laid the halter of his war-mare and a silver *khanjar* in the boy's cradle. The small *khanjar* is a curved dagger, and it was with this very one Nuri had killed in single combat a minor chieftain of the Muntefiq.

One afternoon young Fuaz and a group of his little friends were practising with slings, the ancient weapon with which David slew Goliath. They shot flat pebbles with astounding accuracy at the small wooden pegs, which held the tent ropes down about thirty paces distant. Unseen by them, I suddenly stepped out from behind his tent. A stone, which had hit its target close to me, rebounded from the smooth wood and struck me on the forehead between the eyes. For a moment I was nearly stunned, more perhaps from shock than from the actual blow. My first thought was that I had been struck by a bullet.

Gasping and with a frightened face, Fuaz ran up to me. He had noticed the wound in my forehead and a few drops of blood on my fingers, which I had, in my confusion, pressed to my head. When I took the lad in my arms and laughingly lifted him up, to let him know that it was no great matter, a look of anger crossed his face, as if he had been offended. He wriggled free and stood still before me. Then he tore his *aghal* and *kaffiyah* (the veil and head-cloth) from his head, letting the six fine braids of his hair fall over his shoulders. They reached to his hips. With tears welling from defiant eyes, he cried, *"Ana dachilak!* Before the face of God I deliver myself unto you: tell me the price of your blood." It sounded not in the least regretful, nor did it suggest any wish to be forgiven. It was sheer defiance, because he thought I had made fun of his offer.

How my heart went out to the wild little creature! He had such an air of aloofness and arrogance. Yet it would have been impossible to be angry with him. Was not his whole way of thinking different from a European's? Quite unintentionally he had the blood of his father's guest on his conscience, and he only thought of the satisfaction due to me, before the news of this accident could travel any further. How much blood was shed—in this case only a few drops—did not matter; the only thing that mattered was the unwritten Bedouin law that secures to the stranger absolute safety and inviolability, even in the tent of the humblest nomad. The blood-price of a guest is reckoned twice as high as that of a man killed in fight—fifty camels and four mares.

I had to smile when I thought of the value set on a few drops of my blood. But outwardly I composed my face to due solemnity and, calling the other boys and some men, who had gathered round out of curiosity, as witnesses, I said to Amir Fuaz: "This has happened according to the will of Allah. I know no other price than thy friendship."

For a moment blank amazement! He stared at me wide-eyed. Probably Amir Fuaz could not yet believe it possible that I, a stranger, should invoke the ancient custom of his forefathers. Suddenly he flung away the fateful sling and advanced to me with outstretched arms, and with childish affection he clasped them round my neck as I bent down to him. In a wave of joyous love, I pressed the youngster to my breast and kissed him on both cheeks. With his little finger he lightly dabbed the scratch on my forehead and rubbed four drops of blood on his own forehead between his black eyebrows—the old Bedouin *"Nur-ed-Dam"*, the "Light of Blood."

In this unusual, dramatic fashion I became, by the will of Allah, the blood-brother of Amir Fuaz.

Our friendship was soon to receive baptism by fire. A band of Ruala, two hundred and sixty-eight warriors, led by Rasheyd-ibn-Whafa, set out on a *ghazu* (raid) into the Hamad and the Wudian region, against the Shammar Bedouins, and I accompanied them. We rode twelve hours the first day. In camp that night we were overhauling our riding-gear, water-skins, and so forth, when to our amazement we discovered, curled up in one of the goat-hair camel saddlebags—huge receptacles made of goat skins—little Amir Fuaz, sound asleep.

Not by the slightest sound or sign had he betrayed to us during the long and hard day's ride that we were carrying a stowaway. Our leader, Rasheyd (of the Muraf Ruala), wanted the boy taken home on the morrow by a camel-rider, but Fuaz pleaded so earnestly that the heart of the old freebooter was softened. He merely sent a mounted messenger to Misha'il's camp to let her know that her son was with us.

We were gone on this great *ghazu* almost two months. When we returned, worn out, having suffered serious losses, yet victorious, Amir Fuaz took four of the booty-camels, splendid fawn-coloured beasts, into the camp, and made them kneel before the tent of his blind mother. Misha'il, still a young woman, enquired pleasantly who was the stranger seeking her hospitality. Custom forbade asking direct questions of a stranger. A Rueyli called out: "Khalati—it is a great prince who comes, O blessed daughter, to honour thee."

"And where is his *dira* (pasture) that I may send Hamar, our old slave, to proclaim him to our neighbour?"

"His name is 'The Young Falcon', and his *dira* extends as far as his eyes rove. It is thy son, O mother of Amir Fuaz."

In this foray, Rasheyd, the leader, had his right hand severed by a sword cut. He fainted from loss of blood. Our slaves then plunged the mutilated arm in boiling fat—a desperate remedy but successful, for Rasheyd recovered. He carried his amputated hand from that day forward in the saddle of his racing-camel. It dried up completely, like the hand of a mummy.

When we reached Bahr Saigal, not far from Dumeyr, the first Turkish fortress in Syria, its Commandant sent a cavalry detachment to our camp. He had been informed by telegraph of our illicit operations in the vicinity of the cultivated lands of Mesopotamia. His troopers were seeking Rasheyd, who was to be made answerable. But Rasheyd could not reconcile himself to the prospect of a Turkish dungeon. He placed his withered hand in a leather bag and dictated to Nauaf's *katib* (scribe) the following letter addressed to the Commandant at Dumeyr:

"In the name of the Benevolent and Compassionate! As *askar* (soldier) I cannot serve thy *Padishah* (Sultan), for I have but a stump of an arm. As thy prisoner I could do no work for thee; nay, as a friend I could not even grasp thy hand. What use then being with thee? As a token of my everlasting surrender, however, I offer to thee my hand, since thou art wont to cut off the hand of a thief. Be sure it is my own hand—the hand of Rasheyd-ibn-Whafa, the robber. May God be forbearing with us."

❧ II ❧

Faris—"A Friend of God"

AT THE OUTBREAK of the Great War—I had then already spent three years among the Arabs—I returned to the land of my birth and offered my services
as a volunteer in the German Cavalry. I was, however,
sent to Stamboul and served under the Turkish Crescent
during the fighting at the Dardanelles. Later, I was attached to the Fourth Turkish Brigade on the Suez Canal.
Here, like so many others, I fell a victim to spotted
typhus; but, unlike the majority, I recovered. But my
health was so undermined that I was invalided home.
Apparently Fate had no wish that I should become
mixed up in the desert warfare and politics of the Bedouins. I was laid low again with malaria and an abscess
on the lung, the aftermath of the typhus. In the long
run, the compulsory rest was beneficial. God had blessed
me with an exceptionally tough constitution.

Up to now my history ran as follows: When eighteen
years of age I went to North Africa; a year later I was
in Arabia; then, when I was twenty-one and a half years
old, the scene of my activities was in and about the Dardanelles, followed by a gruelling experience for eight
months near the Suez Canal, which resulted in long
periods of illness. When I celebrated my twenty-fourth
birthday, I was a mere skeleton, my blood reeking with
fever. Though I could scarcely stand on my legs, I expressed my willingness to serve again in Turkey, but the

authorities did not want me there, and instead sent me to Russia, where I spent eighteen months at Prisoners' Clearing Camps. The Armistice found me in the Ukraine, with Germany in collapse and Poland in revolution. Much of all that I had hoped for was lost. Europe held no future for me, and the Near East was closed to Germans. I set out for California and arrived there with one dollar and fifty cents in my pocket, after I had sold my camera and two lenses (faithful companions in many lands) in New York, in order to raise money for the fare to Santa Anna. And here, in this land of milk and honey, of fruit and sunshine, I could look forward to a happy and healthy new life. Living on a ranch, I spent eight or more hours each day on horseback. Thus I recovered my health and my blood was renewed. By the year 1926 I was indeed a new man, and my thoughts began to wander again to Arabia. The yearning grew and grew—this yearning for my Bedouins. Was Amir Fuaz still alive? How were the Ruala doing? And old Nuri? The day came when the yearning could no longer be resisted.

Indeed, four weeks later I celebrated my reunion with Nuri Sha'lan in Damascus, where he had lived since the end of the Great War. At eighty years of age he was still head of his tribe, although he dwelt in a palace in a city and drew an ample revenue from the French. Lately he became a deputy in the Syrian Parliament. The leadership of his tribe in its desert home he had entrusted to no other than Amir Fuaz, his grandson. The latter's father, Nauaf, and two other sons of Nuri, who were still living at the time of my last stay with the Ruala, had died.

Nuri was very astonished, but very happy, to see me again, well and in high spirits. He led me to his private room, which he had furnished according to his Bedouin taste. It was just like the interior of a Bedouin tent, with its coffee-hearth, its heap of white ashes, its mattresses and a profusion of cushions, which, propped against camel-saddles, were a positive incentive to indolence.

A broad-shouldered hunting-falcon stood on a foot-high perch, one powerful talon hidden under its plumage, ready to strike. Nuri removed its leather hood. Great black eyes glared at us and the bird crooned. Then old Nuri called for a pigeon and threw it into the air. With a movement swift as lightning, too swift for the eye to follow, the falcon pounced upon its prey and ripped it open.

Cruelty is inseparable from the Bedouin. He enjoys seeing blood flow. Old Nuri seemed to renew his youthful ardour as he played thus with his falcon. In this world the strong do not always fight with the strong; the weak are so often victims of sheer brutality. In Arabia, in particular, this can never be forgotten.

A week later I resumed my journey. Nuri had given me, as travelling companion and guard, Faris ibn Naif es-Sa'bi, a young Shammar Bedouin, so that I might make my way unmolested to the old chief's great tribe in the neighbourhood of Wadi Sirhan and the red sand of the far-off Nufud desert.

It was curious that a Shammar should act as my conductor to the Ruala, for these tribes have been bitter, nay deadly, enemies for centuries. But the family of Faris had, because of a blood-feud, been living with the Ruala for the past sixteen years. This accounted for the fact that a Shammar could act as my protector in the territory of his tribe's deadly enemies; but the choice also displayed Nuri's wisdom. Being a Shammar, Faris could safeguard me with the enemies of the Ruala, while as Nuri's confidant, he could answer for me before every Rueyli.

Faris was an exceptional man. From the moment of our first meeting, when Nuri introduced him to me, I felt that this must be more than a mere chance acquaintance. The softness of his voice, as he wished me "Peace", and the grip of his strong, manly hand in an instant disclosed to me the open and pure soul of the young Bedouin. Under his hair-cloth cloak beat a heart so affectionate, yet so stout, that I must confess I have never encountered its like among the children of men. To his last breath he was the truest friend I have ever known. Faris was also one of the handsomest men I have ever met. His noble, oval face was unforgettable, with its gentle, dark eyes. His wonderful hair and beard, his flowing shepherd's cloak, made him a striking figure. Tender and gentle as he was, Faris was yet among the boldest and bravest of Ishmaelites. Perhaps he was living two thousand years too late.

After we had left the old suburbs of Damascus behind us, our way led through walnut, olive and apricot orchards into the great open spaces. Majestically the snow-capped peaks of the Syrian mountains rose into the brilliant blue of the skies. Bumpy, dried mud-paths ran through the bare fields and thin, grey meadows. Then came rolling plains, across which ran a puzzling confusion of paths. On the edge of the steppe stood a Syrian Custom's station, where our passports were examined. At last we could leave the overland route; and now, without paths or signposts to guide us, we were in the uncharted desert. Our automobile raced over the hard, dry, pebble-strewn soil, ever eastward, along a never-ending, narrow tongue of land that seemed to dip deeper and deeper into a boundless, shimmering sea. A cloudless sky rose above us and on either side were misty gleams of water over which the air quivered. Suddenly, like apparitions out of the haze, appeared some Arab sheep-breeders. They had but few camels and horses with them, but they rode on asses—a sign of their decadence. They were Fua're. We noticed them as we bore away towards a sheet of water glistening in an elongated depression of the desert.

Mirages were frequent and often incredibly deceptive. Only with difficulty was it possible to distinguish the real rain pools, which were only a foot or so deep with their surfaces ruffled by the wind, from the phantom pools, whose surfaces would be smooth and glassy. Suddenly we noticed ahead of us numerous flocks of sheep. Almost breast-deep they were crossing the flooded land. Automatically I reduced speed, for I suddenly saw, not a hundred yards ahead, a gleam of water—a shallow lake—and we were driving straight into it. I twisted the steering-wheel round, and then only did I realize that what we saw was a dry trough filled with hot, glassy air. At full speed I drove into it towards the rain pools.

Nearer and nearer came the sheep, when in an instant the whole picture changed. The long, wide pool had disappeared; not a trace of moisture was to be seen. Instead of gleaming waters, we saw milling around us a dusty mass of woolly beasts—thousands upon thousands of sheep and goats.

I stopped the car to let the animals pass. The shepherds rode over to us with their women and children, scrutinized us curiously and wished us peace. I distributed cigarettes and sweets, and in response the talkative nomads told us they were moving back to their home-pastures in the north, because other Bedouin tribes had disputed their territory with them. They passed on and the desert became empty again.

The Hamad lay before us, the North-Arabian uplands that seemed to extend into infinity: flat, hard soil, with nothing of any significance to break its level monotony for hundreds of miles southward and eastward. As we sped along, hour after hour, through this parched tableland, immense flocks of migratory birds would whir up out of the camel-grass at our approach. They would fly some hundreds of yards before setting again, like a cloud, upon the earth. Again and again we started clumsy, desert bustards, and large coveys of pintail grouse took wing. These desert birds—about as large as a European partridge—feed mainly on the flaming red caterpillars, which are to be found on every blade and stalk in the otherwise arid waste. Once a small wolf broke cover and two foxes loped away into the distance.

We also came across a huge owl, which sat blinking and bewildered by the daylight, and we brought our car to a standstill close beside it.

Unexpectedly, just before sunset, we had a shower of rain which greatly refreshed the dusty desert. The greater part of the night we passed stretched out on the bare sands in the shelter of a dry river-bed.

On the evening of the following day, after driving like mad, with a sand-storm on our heels, we came up with the Ruala. The great tribe was migrating northward in a body, its encampment sprawling beyond the range of vision, its vast herds spread out in all directions. A shallow depression held one cluster of some eighty tents of all sizes, their open fronts facing to leeward; and among them stood out the most spacious pavilion in Arabia, the famous tent of Nuri Sha'lan.

We drew up there, and my first question was for Amir Fuaz; but the young leader of the Ruala was not at home; he was on a visit to a clan, camping some distance from the main body.

❧ III ❧

The Lone Shepherdess

FARIS AND I set out next morning on horseback; for the headman of the camp had lent us two mares.

With the rustle like that of silk, the delicate stems of wild lavender and camomile broke under the hoofs of the horses. We rode all day. All around us, over low, rain-swept hills and wide levels, stretched the steppe. Not a sign of man; no Bedouins on trek, no herdsmen grazing their beasts; only the wonder of the virgin desert.

Westward the setting sun beamed on us from between thunder-clouds. The darkening East quivered with sheet lightning; distant thunder muttered; and some grey rags of cloud drove before the evening wind as night fell.

As we drew rein on a hill-top, there came from above a sound as of the beat of giant wings. It was the warm wind, driving before it a spring shower. Sadha, my mare, cocked her ears inquisitively. Restlessly she danced and pawed the ground, bent her head and whinnied softly. Then she shook her thick mane, whipped her tail against her thin flanks and thrust her head up. Her senses, keen as a hound's, had made a discovery.

On lightly stepping feet she trotted forward, ears pricked, nostrils wide, making for a small fire that suddenly became visible to us between the mingled shadows of the sky and earth. A fresh scurry of rain obliterated it for a moment. When it had passed we saw also a flock of rain-drenched sheep tightly huddled together. Two huge dogs, barking furiously, challenged our approach. From near the fire came a clear female voice: "Who is there?"

Using my wet hands as a speaking-trumpet, I shouted against the wind as loudly as I could: "Friends!"

"And who is with you?"

"Only God," I replied.

"His countenance be upon you, and peace," the voice answered.

A Bedouin maiden stepped forth from a diminutive tent, calling her dogs to heel, as Faris and I dismounted. She took our horses, placed before them a bowl of milk, and gave us permission to come to the fire. It crackled cheerily, though heavy raindrops were still falling, filling the air with acrid smoke. The pigmy habitation beside the fire hardly deserved the name of tent: it was a single piece of coarse goat-hair cloth, a mere rain-screen, at most affording precarious shelter to the shepherdess and her dogs. A lamb and its mother, which had a broken leg, had taken refuge in it. I set and bound the limb with a few twigs and a gauze bandage, the girl meanwhile watching my manipulations with eager eyes.

She must have been sixteen years of age—a beautiful creature, mature, and lithe, like all Bedouin women. Healthy blood glowed in her sun-bronzed cheeks. Her thick, smooth hair and the high-bridged nose betokened the pure-bred Ishmaelite.

In accordance with the immemorial custom of the

desert, she set before us a bowl of fresh ewe's milk and, turning to me first, said: "Swear to thy sister that no harm will come to her." She gazed at me with large trustful eyes. Her white teeth flashed, and small dimples danced in her cheeks. Taking a dried twig from the brushwood pile by the fire, she held it out to me and said: "Take this in thy hand and swear by the life of the Lord, the giver of all life."

I quickly did her bidding and solemnly pledged the sanctity of her hospitality in the oath no child of the desert would break—an ancient Ishmaelite formula:

"In the name of God: as He took the life from this piece of dead wood, thus may the Lord take life from me if I do not honour and protect thy soul and thy body, O my sister!"

After Faris, too, had taken this oath, she was encouraged to offer us the freedom of her "house" and spread before us all her store of food—bread, fresh milk, a little butter, and dried dates. While Faris and I were supping, she dragged up to the tent a lamb, bleating pitifully and struggling to get free. When I leaned down to hold the animal fast, the girl drew my dagger from my belt and cried: "Kill me this victim, so that I may cook it for thee."

I took the curved blade from her hand and set the frightened lamb free to skip back to the flock. But the maiden looked at me reproachfully.

"All that is needful for sustaining life," I said to her, "thou hast already given to the strangers. Allah is witness, we could not consume a whole lamb. Nor, indeed, can I see any vessel in which its meat could be cooked."

"But here," she said, "is a spit; on it I could roast the kidneys and loin pieces."

Fortunately the girl stood in such horror of killing the animal herself that Faris and I found it easy to convince her that the sacrifice was needless. All she feared was the reproach of her father for not according us Bedouin hospitality in full measure.

Without more words she sat down before the tent and made herself a small fire, that lit up her figure as she bent over it. The flickering light played over her comely face glistening with raindrops. She made a lovely picture of wild, unspoiled beauty and health.

When it became clear to us that the young shepherdess meant to pass the night unsheltered in the open and the rain, I urged her repeatedly not to be afraid and to share the tent with us. I even threatened that if she would not, Faris and I would ride on. But she did not take my threat seriously: she laughed and replied lightly that she could go to her father's tent and come back in the morning.

"Who is thy father?" Faris broke in.

"I am Tuëma, daughter of Sha'il ibn Surhan: and we pitch our tent with the *ashira* (clan) of the Freyje."

"Tuëma," said Faris coaxingly, "it is far to thy father's place and it is night. Do thou trust us and repose thyself here at our feet."

"Truly, I am not afraid," the girl said at last; "stay with me and do not ride on." She rose as she spoke, flung a handful of faggots on the fire, and waited for the flames to leap up. Then she straightened her magnificent young body to its full height and, slipping the cloak

· 22 ·

from her shoulders, came into the tent. She stood facing us while she undid her wet neckcloth, both her tapering arms with their delicate wrists stretched high above her head, seemingly quite at ease; only her dark eyes regarded us somewhat shyly.

I had stretched myself out in the shelter of the tent-cloth. Close behind me the crippled mother-ewe and her lamb had bedded down; they had found a warm spot against my shoulder and my fur-lined cloak.

Faris, who had been lying at my side, jumped up when the girl entered and helped her to spread her wet shepherd's cloak over a tilted tent-pole. When she had made up a "bed" for herself and was lying down, Faris spread his own shepherd's cloak over her. The girl protested; but he pointed to his *farwa* (fur caftan) and warm bedding of sheepskins and she let him have his way, casting a friendly glance at him. Both Faris and I were concerned not to disturb Tuëma's trust in us by word or deed.

The rain cleared and the silent moon rose. Its tender light shone on the gentle slopes of distant hills, while a warm wind fanned the steppe, drying grasses and flowers, the shivering sheep and our wet tent-wall.

Tuëma and Faris were sound asleep, as I could tell from their rhythmic breathing. I lay musing between waking and sleeping.

Suddenly the dogs started to bark furiously. In a trice Faris was up, had drawn his pistol from its holster and had rushed out. But even before he could pass beyond the shadow of the tent, Tuëma had reached him and had flung her arms round his body. "Thou wilt scare the flock," she cried warningly; "do not shoot. It is only some small wolves; my dogs will chase them away. . . . Sushan! Kasabi!" she shouted, as she urged on the dogs.

Faris lowered his pistol. Tuëma took it out of his hand and replaced it in his belt; but she did not release him. Timidly she pressed herself against him, her arms about his hips. Her garments fluttered faintly, stirred by the warm dry breeze. The steppe exhaled its perfume. The air was saturated with a scent like that of lavender. Dawn had come, revealing the woolly backs of the huddled sheep, now quiet again. From far away, growing fainter and fainter, came the barking of the dogs, still chasing the wolves. Close by, our tethered horses snorted.

Faris gently disengaged himself from Tuëma's arms and, taking her by the hand, led her to the tent, where they sat down side by side. As he leant towards her and kissed her on the top of the head, Tuëma drew the curved poniard from his belt and put it in her lap.

"Let this dagger rest in my lap," said she. It was thus she reminded him of her virginity. Among Bedouins of pure race, a girl's chastity has been, and still is, the most sacred rubric in the tribal code of honour. For its violation a father may kill his daughter, a brother his sister, and have her flesh cut in pieces.

The sun broke through the veils of the morning, shooting flaming fingers across the heavens, and the dark earth glowed rosily. "Sabah!" whispered Faris to his beloved. *Sabah* means the morning, but it is also a poetic word for "virgin bride." Tuëma leaned her cheek to his.

So they sat, motionless, without a word. Then Tuëma

rose silently and strode toward her flock, but stopped suddenly and stood still. Entranced, Faris's eyes drank in the beauty of her figure, clearly outlined beneath the folds of her thin garments, glorified by the rays of the morning sun. But when he started to follow, she gave a laugh and drawing her cloak about her shoulders, ran off swiftly to the depression where her sheep were grazing and her dogs played, rolling over each other in the luxuriant herbage.

The radiance of a flawless morning was over the wilderness. In the crystal-clear air the eye could sweep far horizons across an immense succession of tawny hills and green glades. A few fleecy clouds sailed in the blue heavens. A lark rose, jubilant, soaring higher and higher in an ecstasy of melody. And over the steppe, like a caress, still moved the gentle, warm wind.

Such was the morning on which love awakened in Faris's heart.

Breakfast; and then Faris and I must resume our ride. Tuëma rekindled the fire on the hearth, stirred some flour into cold water, shaped the dough into small thin loaves, and baked them on the glowing ashes. During the meal she dipped dates into butter, rolled each into a piece of the still warm bread, and fed these morsels alternately into Faris's mouth and mine.

"Wilt thou ever return?" Tuëma asked her new-found lover.

"All is known to the Lord," replied Faris wistfully.

"And wilt thou think of me?"

"And thou?"

For answer she took him by the hand and led him to our horses. When Faris had swung himself on to the back of his mare, she hid her face against his thigh and began to weep. Leaning down, he gently raised her head by the chin and looked deep into her eyes. As her lifted face yearned towards him, their lips met for the first time. Her long eyelashes swept his cheek.

And Faris told me later:

"I felt her shining teeth when my lips left her lips; it was like the taste of milk."

"Stay!" Tuëma cried after us.

"God be my witness," Faris called back, "that henceforward thy love will be the inseparable companion of my heart."

"Peace be with thee, O Faris."

As often as we looked back, we could see Tuëma standing motionless by her flock, gazing after us. On the last hillock Faris unwound his *kaffiyah* (head-cloth) and waved it to the dwindling figure of the girl. She fluttered her shepherd's cloak in answer.

⚙ IV ⚙

I Meet My Blood Brother Again

PEACE AND HAPPINESS smiled on the world. Here and there a rain pool still shone in a hollow; wind and sun had already dried the hill-crests. A whirlwind rose ahead of us: it swept the ground like a broom; uprooted, snapped, and scattered small plants and flowers, and left behind it a narrow zigzag track, like that of a monstrous snake. We were coated with a dust of fine sand and pollen. Crickets chirped in the herbage. Bustards and pintail grouse were busily hunting for woolly red caterpillars. Suddenly and quite unexpectedly, on topping a rise, we caught sight of black tents at the foot of the opposite slope. Very soon now I should see Amir Fuaz again.

The tent of ceremony in which, long exciting years before, I had enjoyed Nauaf's hospitality and had come to know his small son, was pitched far from the place on which it stood then. Yet everything seemed the same. I felt myself spirited back to that time and place. There were the same far-scattered lines of low black tents, open in front; the same camel-herds stringing out into the endless desert under the brilliant sun. The cushioned camel-saddle in the guest-tent against which I reclined, the very fire on the hearth where the coffee-water was steaming, looked the same; and the women's quarters in the tent, with its disarray of saddles, saddlebags, mattresses, cushions and what not, seemed to be just as I had last seen it.

On the left of the guest-tent stood a smaller tent. From it presently emerged a young Bedouin, simply clad, but attended by four slaves carrying hunting-hawks, a string of greyhounds beside them. As I went to meet him, I had an absurd sense of unreality. I knew, of course, who he was, but at the moment I simply could not feel that this dignified manly *sheykh* ceremoniously advancing towards me was really the playful little boy of yore, the lovable but dirty gamin we had one night dragged out of a camel saddlebag. Of one thing, however, I was instantly aware: Fuaz did not know me; and my name, as Arabian guest-ceremonial demands, had so far remained unspoken, nor had any news of my coming preceded me.

A Negro slave placed a small *ekim*—a black rug with a coloured border design—at my feet. On this small but sacred emblem the Amir and I exchanged greetings. With his right hand over his heart he bade me "God's peace." Then he conducted me within the guest-tent.

The four slaves spread the precious tribal rug of state: it covered the whole floor. On the farther side of the hearth, a great pile of sheepskins, rugs, and cushions, buttressed against two camel-saddles, made a luxurious divan—the throne of the desert chieftain. Fuaz slipped off his sandals and motioned to me to seat myself on his right. Notables, slaves, and men of the Amir's body-guard ranged themselves on the great rug. No one spoke.

All eyes were on the coffee-cook, who raked together the smouldering embers on the hearth and added new dried camel dung. On the silence soon fell the sound of boiling water bubbling in the capacious long-spouted pot.

The Amir's body-servant, Mnahi—the same who had spread the rug of greeting—took a stick of incense from a fold of his head-cloth, broke off a piece and placed it on a glowing dung-ember. Through the black roof-cloth filtered faintly the sunshine and wove a pattern of lights and shadows on the ground. Courtiers, warriors, and slaves formed a solemn, silent semicircle. Facing these squatting figures, Mnahi alone was on his feet; he had taken his post on his master's left and stood there, erect and motionless, one sinewy black fist on the silver hilt of his sword.

I stole surreptitious glances at my host. His *kaffiyah* framed an effeminate type of face, oval, with regular features and a high-bred, slightly aquiline nose. The dark eyes, brilliant and very large, were set beneath wide thick brows and a rather narrow forehead. When he smiled, dazzling white teeth showed under the small black moustache. The more I looked at this romantic young man, the more I recognized in him that spirited little blood-brother of mine in the long ago. It required an effort of will to restrain my impatience and not to declare myself forthwith; but I had to await the fitting moment. So far, no one had uttered a word. All seemed to be interested exclusively in the cook, still puttering about his hearth. In desert etiquette it is a gross breach of courtesy to ply a guest with questions about himself.

At length, however, Fuaz gave me the longed-for opening; he turned to me suddenly and said: "Whencesoever thou comest, O stranger, be thou welcome here!"

"O Amir Fuaz," I replied, "stranger I can hardly be called among thy people. For once upon a time, in this very tent, I knew a boy, then little taller than the sword under thy slave's hand. And it came to pass one afternoon, when that boy and his playmates were shooting with the sling, that I, by the will of God, chanced to walk near; and a pebble flung by that child's hand struck me squarely between the eyes. Now, one might have said that Allah had marked my forehead with the *Nur-ed-Dam* (Seal of Blood). Therefore demanded I a great price for my blood."

Fuaz, who had listened with head inclined and lowered eyes, as if pondering, now raised them impetuously. For a moment he stared at me as in a trance. Then his face lit up; with a shout of joy he leapt to his feet, seized me by the shoulders, and strained me to his breast. "Aziz," he cried, using the Arab name bestowed on me by his tribe in the days of his childhood, "Aziz, thou art returned! *El-hamdu l'illah!*"

Again and again he kissed me on the cheeks and embraced me. "Now," he said, "do I understand the words I learned from my *mu'allim* (teacher): thou who followest with thy eye the flight of a bird or the course of the pebble flung from thy hand, what knowest thou of God's purposes?"

Yes, I had returned!

Once more I was with my Bedouins, to migrate again with their herds, to lie under their humped tent-roofs, to cover league after league perched on a racing-camel under the sun and the stars, to gallop astride one of their blue-blooded mares, those "Drinkers of the Wind", with slim greyhounds racing on the flanks of our cavalcade.

☙ V ☙

Love in the Desert

I T WAS A SEASON of great fertility here in the south by
the Wadi Sirhan. Thunder showers and rain all over
the land. The face of the earth had become one great
pasture. The swelling udders of the she-camels oozed
milk. Their calves were legion—comical, clumsy, long-
legged creatures. A medley of sounds filled the air—
mingled with the creaking and groaning of camel litters
on the dromedaries' backs, from under the awnings of
which appeared happy-faced mothers, fondling their
young babies. This was the springtime of the year, when
nature was pulsating with life. Women were being de-
livered of their children in their tents and some even in
the shade, amongst the animals, which were also big with
young. In the low bushes and camel-grass could be heard
the cheeping and chirping of desert chicks and fledg-
ling bustards. The withered old desert had miraculously
renewed herself and had become beautiful again with
the bloom of youth.

The gentle caresses of the rain and the sun had coaxed
out myriads of blossoms. A diaphanous haze, silver and
green, suffused hill and dale. Deeper and richer glowed
the green of the flower-strewn meads in the wide depressions. Scent-laden, the soft spring wind blew gently
over the gracious land. The eyes of the herdsmen were
bright with gratitude; yet, morning after morning, the
women would pull the tent-posts from under the

buckled roofs, roll up the unwieldy goat-hair tents and load them on the sturdy camels.

Of that time, when the sun was moving northward and the tribe was moving with it—a time when Faris went to see his betrothed nearly every day—one memory stands out in high relief.

"Let us go hunting," Faris said to me one morning, and bade Mnahi hand him the automatic hunting-rifle which I had given him as a keepsake. We went to our horses, which stood patiently between the lines, loosed their halters, and vaulted on to their backs. Then we cantered out into the plain.

As we swept across a hill-top, we saw, a long way off, a good-sized herd of gazelles in full career and heading straight toward us. From time to time the animals disappeared from sight in a hollow, but as they came nearer, we saw that they were in flight from a Bedouin, pursuing them on a swift sorrel mare. He was plainly seeking to cut out a pure white buck, the leader of the herd. Again and again the buck found safety by pushing into the midst of his racing mates; but the sorrel was nimble of foot and well-trained, and her rider skilful. The herd repeatedly broke and scattered; and the pursuer steadily gained on his prey. At last he fired at close range and the gazelle-buck tumbled over and over and lay still.

When we had come closer to the hunter, who was already dressing his game, we noticed with amazement that it was no man at all. "By my faith, it is a maiden," cried Faris. We urged on our horses, and I was the first to come up with the huntress. She had risen, the blood-stained knife in one hand; with the other she pulled her neckerchief up to her eyes, to hide her features. But I had already recognized her. "Tuëma!" I called out delightedly. For a moment she showed only her laughing eyes; then she let the neckcloth drop from her face and held out both hands to me. I drew her to me and kissed her on the forehead.

Faris, still in the saddle, pretended to be greatly astonished. "Aziz," he exclaimed, with perfect dissimulation, "dost thou know this maiden?"

Taking up his jest, I shook my head. "No; but she looks very much like one I know."

But love's impatience cut short the little comedy. Faris slipped from his horse and embraced Tuëma, babbling his delight at meeting her so unexpectedly. Then he took one of her hands and laid it in mine, saying: "This is thy sister, O Aziz; and if she were not my betrothed, she might well be thine. Is it not so, Tuëma?" She nodded bashfully.

When Faris helped her to tie the buck on her mare's crupper, I noticed with surprise that the animal did not shy at the smell of blood. Faris had trained it, Tuëma explained. He had taken the mare on a raid and had only recently sent her to Tuëma's father as a bride-gift. She was a *muhajjala* and he had named her Sabah on account of her colour—a sorrel with a white blaze and white stockings on the forelegs. The beautiful beast whinnied softly and rubbed her forehead on Tuëma's shoulder. "She is coaxing you," said Faris.

With a few vigorous and dexterous strokes of her hunting-knife Tuëma severed head and neck from the buck's carcass and handed me the bloody trophy. Then she picked up her carbine and, like a boy, vaulted on the back of her horse with a single swing over its flank and a twist of her body. She gave us a roguish parting look and rode off.

Faris gripped me hard by the shoulder. "She is as shy as a gazelle fawn," he exclaimed ecstatically. "And can there be another maid as beautiful as she?"

The following day Faris fetched me to go on a visit to Tuëma's household. After we had exchanged compliments with her father, Surhan, we went to the women's quarters. Tuëma was there alone; the other inmates of the harem had gone out.

Faris put his arms about his beloved. "My wild he-ostrich," she greeted him, nestling her head on his shoulder. "My little ostrich-hen," he replied.

Tuëma presently handed her lover one of the Bedouin bread-loaves, which was twisted together in the manner of a dumpling. It contained a small sugary cake of Tuëma's own making, the traditional offering of an espoused Bedouin maiden to her husband-to-be. Faris broke it into three pieces, sharing it with the girl and me. He thanked her gravely and then, stroking her hair, he said: "In exchange for this I shall gather for thee a bouquet that shall not wither, and I shall bring thee also a pair of silver ankle-rings."

Tuëma laughed and held out her hand. "No bigger than the tip of my little finger are the flowers of our wilds, and thou dost promise to pick a bouquet for me? And where wouldst thou find silver bangles where there is no silversmith?"

"In truth, loveliest maid, O my mistress, I shall pick for thee a bunch of rare flowers wherewith to adorn thyself for our festive hours in the hills," he insisted.

Still incredulous, she mocked at him, gaily rumpling his head till she had pulled off his *aghal* and *kaffiyah*.

"Oh, how untidy thou art!" she exclaimed.

Six dishevelled tresses had tumbled over his shoulders. She drew him closer and put his head in her lap. Then she set about rebraiding in proper fashion his Ishmaelite locks. From the flap of her head-cloth she took a handful of dried gazelle dung; small blackish-green capers. They spread an odour of thyme and camomile as she crumbled the pellets between her palms and rubbed the stuff, like a scent-powder, into the long strands of hair. Faris kept as still as a mouse, without a word.

At last she had completed her task. Faris replaced his head-dress; then he declared: "Now it is the turn of Aziz!"

Whether I would or no, I too must put my head in Tuëma's lap and let her, with Faris's assistance, plait my mop into little pigtails and powder them with her exotic perfume. What a sight I must have looked! I always regret that I did not have my photograph taken then. At all events, Faris and Tuëma grew so merry over their handiwork that people from the neighboring tents came running up and burst out laughing at "Aziz Radhwan."

As Faris and I were leisurely riding homeward that night, we heard distant hoof-beats behind us. The sound rapidly grew, and there came a rush of riders—twelve or more Bedouins on swift steeds. In the moonlight I saw their long locks and head-cloths fluttering, their shepherd's cloaks flapping in the air. They noticed us and came straight towards us. As they galloped past, they brandished their carbines and boisterously called out our names. We urged on our horses and sped after them to the tent of the chieftain.

⚜ VI ⚜

The Commander of Our Camel-Saddles

WHEN WE DREW rein, slaves were already lighting a huge signal-fire to call together the warriors of the tribe. A strong raiding-party of the Bishri (the three federated clans of the Anaza: the Fid'an, Saba, and Amarat) was reported to be advancing. It was said to number five hundred camel-riders, with some hundreds of war-mares. Perhaps the numbers were exaggerated.

That night Amir Fuaz made all his dispositions. Before the first grey of dawn Faris was at my bedside. "Awake, if thou wouldst ride with us," I heard him say, with a laugh. I jumped up and hastened to make ready for the march. Faris handed me a filled water-skin, a lump of pressed dates, several balls of hard Bedouin cheese, the size of a fist, and a stack of fresh-baked bread-cakes. With the help of Mnahi, who was to be my rider-attendant, I stowed everything in the saddlebags of my *dhalul* (racing-camel), saddled Sadha, my white war-mare, and tied her by her halter to the dromedary's cinch.

Amir Fuaz had appointed Faris leader of our camel corps.

It was still dark when we started. The moon had set. The night was calm and the voices of the riders chanting as they rode made no echo, but moved over the desert like a wave of sound—eerie, magic, beautiful. In the darkness loomed the indistinct figures of the camels; now and then only was heard the faint padding of soft soles, or the creak of a saddle. Thus, like riders from another world, we made our noiseless way among the hills, till dawn broke over them and at last the sun rose.

Slender, silver chains, braided girths, and coloured halters, embroidered with blue and red beads, adorned the necks and flanks of our camels. At their sides cantered the riderless mares, necks gently arched, supple backs taut, tails high—held only by the gay-coloured top-piece of the woollen headgear; for the Bedouins of Arabia, in contrast to the African, use neither bit nor bridle. The thin saddle-cloths were made of panther or gazelle skins, secured by a narrow leather girth.

Like wildcats, with glittering eyes and taut muscles, the companion-riders crouched behind their comrades on the high humps of the camels, carbines at the ready. From their shoulders floated the ends of their *kaffiyahs*, which they wore wound about head and neck.

In the early afternoon, Faris, riding at our head in the midst of his black bodyguard, gave the signal to change mounts; he had seen a dust cloud which, it appeared, was caused by two automobiles now approaching rapidly.

In the twinkling of an eye, sixty-seven fierce fellows had flung themselves, rifle in hand, from their trotting dromedaries to the backs of their mares and had unslipped the lines from the camel-girths. Then they dug their bare heels into their horses' flanks, and leaving the camel-troop behind, forged ahead and were lost in a cloud of dust. Only their wild yells, the neighing of their horses, and the drumming of the hoofs were audible. The mad rush of the horsemen had made Sadha, my mare, restive; she pulled at her line and gave me to understand that she wanted to be in it too. I grabbed my Mauser and vaulted from the high saddle of my *dhalul* to her back. With a whinny she responded to the pressure of my thighs and careened after the others, extending herself like a gazelle when I, with my face almost touching her mane, called her by name. Closer and closer to the band thundering ahead she carried me, and soon I had overtaken the rearmost and was coming up with Faris and his escort.

The automobiles now appeared on a ridge and we recognized them at once as battle-cars of the Ruala. We all stopped and waited for their coming. It turned out that they carried Amir Fuaz himself, accompanied by Mijhem and several other men. They had captured in the neighborhood of their camp a scout of the Beni Sakhr. This man had refused to answer questions, and the Amir had forbidden his men to force information from him by torture; yet from the appearance of the spy in that locality, the young chieftain thought it reasonable to infer that the tribe of the Beni Sakhr had also taken arms against the Ruala, who were threatened from the other side as well by the Bishri. He therefore divided our force: two thirds, now under the command of Mijhem, were to remain facing the Bishri; the other third, under Faris, was to swing southeast against the Beni Sakhr.

Naturally, I attached myself to Faris's command. Before we parted from the others, I purchased a magnificent racing-camel six years old, which its owner, a Rueyli, had looted from the Sharrarat; a fawn she-*dhalul* with a lion's head and great gazelle eyes. I had fallen in love with this fine animal at first sight. She was the pride of her captor and she cost me more than I had ever dreamed of paying for a racing-camel—sixty-five pounds sterling—but she was worth the money.

What was most beautiful in her and what charmed me most were the long, ideal line of the back and the high-swung belly-line from the breastbone to the hind thighs. This racing build gave her ample freedom for paces which were a sheer delight—even and soft, easy and long-striding. She was very speedy and indefatigable in either trot or gallop, as I proved the very day I bought her. It was pure joy to be privileged to ride this thoroughbred animal; I had not been deceived in her.

She was small, but had extraordinary endurance, though she was often overtaxed. Despite her size and light build and fine bones, she was a great load-carrier. In vigour she was equal to the very biggest and strongest racing-camels. Without losing a scrap of her elegance and good looks, this noble animal carried me for weary weeks on the long ride into the Nufud and back. Her satin skin never lost its lustre. Even her sweet breath was more pleasing than that of any other of the many racing-camels I have known. Her hips, neck and legs were slim; her hump small, but firm; her voice soft and tender, a low gurgling or sobbing. But as a rule she would converse with me by means of her speaking eyes or a gentle push with her nose against my shoulder or thigh. She loved to rub herself against me and to play with me; and at night, chewing her cud, she would snuggle and bend so cleverly that I had a comfortable, sheltered bed-place against her warm body.

She was sumptuously caparisoned. Her *shedad*, the silver-mounted saddle of acacia wood, with its leather cushions and three sheepskins, still rests on the floor of my room; and often of an evening I sit on it and read, or dream of Maha, the fleet Sharrarijeh. On the wall of my room hangs, wonderfully preserved, her saddle trappings and the huge goat-hair saddlebags, with long rows of knotted tassels and braided fringes that used to reach far below Maha's belly and swing in rhythm with her gait. Her *rashma*, too, I still have—the head-halter of fine, coloured wool—red, blue, and green on a black background.

Shouting merrily to one another and singing camel-songs, we trotted southward. In Arabia neither spurs nor whips are needed for urging on horses or camels. The riders' cheerful, rhythmic chants, their merry yodeling, their clear melodious voices, suffice. The Arab voice is very unlike the nasal, sleepy, monotonous croak of the Egyptians and Syrians. The Bedouin camel-songs are masculine, bold, and tuneful, so that the camels and the horses love this diversion. On the march these hardy, lean riders will sing hour after hour. But often enough they will be silent, when hunger, thirst, and dust have wearied them, or when it is expedient to muffle mouth and nose from the heat and sand.

❧ VII ❧

Death in the Desert

FARIS AND HIS band marched along in high spirits. The sky was blue, the earth a verdant green, the scented air full of sunshine; and from horizon to horizon stretched the wilderness in one unbroken expanse.

At times one lost the sense of progress. Were we standing still? Riding in a circle?—so unchanging was the landscape. Yet one never tired of it, nor could one have enough of this exhilarating motion.

Steppe, desert, rising and falling imperceptibly; ridge hardly distinguishable from valley; except, perhaps, that the valley still glistened a little from the last shower and showed a more vigorous touch of fresh green.

Three days we thus journeyed. For three days no tents, no herds; nothing but the empty wilderness under the serene sky; now gay with herbage, now grim with gravel, stones, and lava.

On the fourth day, from the edge of a steep escarpment, as from a sea-cliff, we suddenly saw spread before our eyes the Wadi Sirhan, here immensely wide. A medley of chalk-coloured banks rising from lime rock, stony plains, salt marshes, sand dunes, grey shrubs, tablelands, deep-furrowed, loamy beds of rain torrents, called *wudian,* covered with black rubble.

Towards the evening of the next day we reached Mayku', an old watering-place of the Ruala. Some hundreds of them were still under tents there in the shadow of the grey hills, and we bivouacked with them. All through the night they kept watering their herds at the deep well-holes, and we heard the incessant creaking of the small wooden rollers in the primitive wooden bearings, with their dripping ropes, some eighty feet long.

A few hours' ride beyond Mayku' we entered the wide dark tableland of Bsayta, the flattened remains of what is probably the oldest mountain range in the Arabian peninsula. A few inconsiderable summits, covered with a fine film of sand, still rise from its surface, which extends for more than sixty miles—a perfectly level waste without water, without pasture, on which it seems to have hailed black gravel. At one stroke the blithe world was changed; all round us was desolation. But gloomy and eerie as Bsayta appeared at first sight, a few days in it taught me to love this waste, with all its hopeless melancholy. The solitude and stillness as of an abandoned planet broded over it. Now and then an oryx-antelope or an ostrich fled at our approach. Very rarely did we pass a shrub that was knee-high or see a green leaf or a flower. No bird sang here; even snakes and lizards avoided this waste. Occasionally in summer, it depended on the rainfall, there grew a strange, rich crop in Bsayta —the *samh,* a low small-leaved plant, on whose twigs small berries ripen, containing reddish-brown seed granules. These the Bedouins roast and grind into a dark, bitter flour. Kneaded with sheep butter and dates, or boiled in water into a sort of porridge, it becomes edible.

After renewing our water supply at the Hausa well, we pushed on toward Bir Bair and into the northwestern Wadi Sirhan, the proper grazing grounds of the Beni

Sakhr. One after another we reconnoitred the scattered camps of our supposed enemy, despatching after each such reconnaissance two couriers with messages to our main body, which was then camping near the Umm Wual. One night Faris himself, "Commander of our Camel-saddles", as we called him, crept close enough to the tents of the Beni Sakhr to be able to listen to their talk. The total result of our efforts seemed to be the comforting conclusion that the Beni Sakhr must have given up their plans for a raid on the Ruala.

We preserved caution, however; and one morning, soon after sunrise, as we were lying in ambush on the salt-crusted ground under cover of some bushes, long lines of free camels appeared on the plain and scattered to graze. Behind them came loaded camels and migrating families of the Beni Sakhr. We hoped they would make camp before noon, so that we might make sure whether their fighting-men were still with them. But it was already late afternoon when we saw them, from a great distance, halt their camels. Tent-rolls and props tumbled to the ground, and women, children, and slaves industriously started to pitch the new camp. Now there arrived also numerous horsemen and camel-riders—the guards who had been covering the flanks of the migrating band.

Almost without sound our *dhaluls* rose as we left our last hiding-place and with long strides trotted after Faris's she-camel. She was pregnant and had been restless all day. Suddenly she refused to go farther and lay down. This spelt danger for us, for scouts always range the vicinity of a Bedouin camp. Moreover, there could be no better place for the enemy to ambush us: white lime rocks shut us in on one side, while the rest was a confusion of blackish glistening scree and bush-crowned clay tumuli.

Several of us helped Faris to unharness his *dhalul*, since it was clear that she would calve. She turned on her side. Faris looked at us crestfallen, as if expecting reproaches; but all merely laughed at this misadventure. There was not a harsh word, no cursing, no blaming of the innocent camel—only that calm and composure of the Bedouin that ever evokes my admiration.

Faris kept tenderly stroking his beloved *dhalul*, and when the moment had come, while I held down the animal's head, he and one of his slaves aided the delivery of the calf. It was as tall as a grown man. At first, I thought it was stillborn, but after its mother had licked it for some time, it gave signs of life. That night the baby camel could stand on its legs and was allowed to suckle; but toward morning it was led aside and killed. The poor mother wailed and moaned loudly for her offspring. But she quieted down when Faris came back to her. She kept nosing his arm and shoulder and sniffing the air. This aroused my curiosity and I went nearer. Faris had sewn a piece of the baby camel's hide on the sleeve and shoulder of his cloak. It was this that had soothed the mother. Later in the afternoon, before we remounted, she let herself be milked. She would still whimper from time to time, but instantly became quiet when Faris reached out his arm or pressed his shoulder to her nostrils.

At length, about noon, we rode forward, our scouts in advance.

Beyond a ridge we saw vultures circling. At the foot of its farther slope we found trampled ground and the dead bodies of a Bedouin and his riding-camel. The man's body had been stripped. Not a scrap of clothing could we find, neither saddle nor gear, to help us find out whence he had come and of what tribe he was.

One of our scouts came back just then to report that camels of the Beni Sakhr were grazing close ahead and that armed guards were with the herdsmen.

Suddenly we caught sight of a number of men on some rising ground, half hidden by the bushes, and the glint of rifles levelled at us. "Ho, there! Ye camel-riders!" they called to us.

"Friends!" Faris shouted back, as we pulled up. But shots cracked and bullets whistled over our heads. Faris laughed. "Beni Sakhr," he exclaimed. "Here stand Ruala. Here stands Faris ibn Naif. Peace—peace unto you!"

But the men did not trust us. It must, indeed, have seemed very suspicious to them that a *ghazu* of the Ruala should appear in so distant a region. They did not return our peace-greeting. Instead, cries of "Kill them! Kill them!" rose from many throats all around us.

New opponents seemed to rise out of the ground. Undoubtedly they had left their horses out of sight and had crept up under cover. At last, just when their shouts of "Kill them" sounded particularly ominous, and shots crackled repeatedly, and we were vainly trying to make ourselves understood in the general hubbub, one man strode from cover and called out: "Faris ibn Naif!"

Our leader slipped from his *dhalul* and called back joyously: "Jirad ibn Jeneyb!" It was one of the *shiyukhs* of the Beni Sakhr, and an old acquaintance of Faris.

In a trice the Beni Sakhr broke cover and pressed about us. We were deluged with questions as they led us to their camp, a few hours' distant. On the way Faris told them of the capture of a scout of their tribe and of our peaceable journey of inquiry into their grazing-grounds. Ever and again Ibn Jeneyb protested that the Beni Sakhr were at "unclouded peace" with the Ruala and that the captured spy must be a robber and an outcast from the tribe, who wanted to plunder the Ruala on his own account.

When we had dismounted in his camp, Ibn Jeneyb had a camel slaughtered before our eyes. A slave caught its blood in a bowl. He then tore up a bunch of herbs, dipped it in the blood, and with this brush painted the tribal emblem on the necks and flanks of our riding-camels. This was to serve, as it were, as a guarantee of our peaceful intentions and as a safe conduct among the rest of the Beni Sakhr.

A small detachment of them were still pursuing Bedouins of the northwestern lava region, who had broken into the Wadi Sirhan and, the day before, had fallen on Beni Sakhr herders, grazing their camels. The raiders lost one dead—it was his corpse we had found—while the Beni Sakhr had two men wounded.

I visited these wounded men and found one of them, with two ghastly bullet wounds in his chest and abdomen, lying at the point of death. I did my best to save him—I had my case of surgical instruments, morphine and bandages with me—but it was too late to help. I could do no more than ease his last hours by alleviating his pain. He could not have been over forty. Friends carried him presently the short distance to Ibn Jeneyb's tent and laid him down there. Then a slave led up a handsome riding-camel. It was touching to see how the intelligent animal seemed to sense that its master was dying. It caressed him repeatedly, and with large, anxious eyes circled round, touching the strange men with its slit lips and its soft silky nostrils.

The dying man was speaking to Ibn Jeneyb, his chieftain, when a severe hæmorrhage caused him to faint. When he came to again, he whispered some words to the slave; and before I could take in what was happening, the Negro, bending back the camel's head, killed it with a lightning plunge of his dagger into the jugular vein.

Other slaves immediately skinned the animal and spread out the hide, the bloody side up, before the tent. Then they undressed the dying man and laid him on it. His last wish had been to be buried in the skin of his cherished *dhalul*, and the thought that his wish was to be realized made him happy as he lay dying. But I was not the only one to regret the purposeless death of the splendid animal.

When, toward evening, the man had breathed his last, four or five of the watchers, his friends, got up, one after another, and lightly touched his forehead with their finger-tips. Ibn Jeneyb, who knelt beside the dead man, put his hand under his left armpit; after a while he called out: "In truth, he is cold!"

Getting up hastily, he folded the wet, bloody winding-sheet over the corpse and directed his slaves to dig a grave for him in the sand. Without ceremony or any show of emotion, it was borne away and given into the keeping of the earth.

After parting from the Beni Sakhr, we moved back by slow marches toward the hill lands of Bir Hausa, which abound in game.

At the wells we fell in with camel-riders watering a herd. They were Sharrarat, and friendly to the Ruala—luckily, as it turned out. They helped us to draw water from the holes fifty feet deep; and in the evening we withdrew with them into the protecting hills, camping in a rocky hollow, with sentries posted on the black pinnacles. The stars sparkled down on us as we ate supper. It consisted of the roasted flesh of a camel calf, very tender, crisp bread-cakes and fresh camel milk, followed by the customary "dessert" of dates mixed with sour sheep butter. It was after midnight before we rolled up in our cloaks, each man with his loaded carbine under his head. For we did not completely trust the Sharrarat, even though we had eaten and drunk together and they lived under Nuri Sha'lan's "heel." But the night passed peacefully, and on the morrow, after we had exchanged trifling presents, we bade good-bye to our hosts.

◈ VIII ◈

Panther and Ostrich

SEVERAL DAYS WERE spent by us among the volcanic table-mountains of the Jabal Tubayk. Precipitous cliffs, riven and pinnacled rocks rise some six hundred feet from flower-sprinkled level pastures and valleys strewn with black lava boulders. It is a country of savage beauty, in which gazelles and game birds are numerous.

There Faris and I, out after game, chanced to come on three tents tucked away in a hollow. They belonged to members of that curious folk, the Sulkan (singular: Sleyb)—nomadic hunters and handicraftsmen. In the popular sense they resemble the gypsies. Like them they doctor man and beast, love music, are fortune-tellers, and have a weakness for things occult and superstitious.

As hunters, trackers and scouts the Sulkan surpass the other Bedouins, and they know the desert better than any other nomads. Many a secluded water-hole is known only to them. Their origin is a mystery. They are few in number, but are held together by some sort of tribal organization, under a chief; and they pay tribute—"protection money"—to the Ruala and other Bedouin tribes. In return, each of these appoints from among its own tribesmen a "Brother" to the Sulkan, charged with looking after their interests.

The Chief of the Sulkan was then one Ralib welde Tulihan, and it was to this young man that the little camp we had discovered belonged. Ralib, accompanied

by his wife and children, and two brothers and their
families, was on his way north to the Ruala (five or six
hundred miles mean nothing to these people) to treat
with his "Brother" there for the recovery of some thirty
Sulkan camels which, he said, a band of unidentified
Ruala had driven off.

One of the tents of these Arab gypsies was made of
sewn gazelle skins. For tent-pegs they used oryx horns.
I observed that these people had no vessels made of wood;
all I saw were of leather. In place of rugs and cushions
they used the skins of asses, ostriches, panthers, and antelopes. Their clothing, too, excepting the shepherd's
cloaks, was made of pelts and hides.

Faris proposed to Ralib that he should guide us into
the Nufud and promised to charge himself with the
matter of the camels and round them up as soon as he
returned to the tribe; Ralib's family, meanwhile, were
to wander northward without him. Ralib accepted; and
soon thereafter we departed from the wild Jabal Tubayk.

We had followed Ralib's lead for several uneventful
days when, on reaching a *wadi*, he pointed out the fresh
tracks of a panther. Leaving our camels behind under
guard, we followed the trail on horseback for some distance, when suddenly our mares snorted through wide-
open nostrils; they had winded the beast of prey. We
dismounted and crept cautiously towards an escarpment,
where Ralib surmised the panther was in hiding. It had
been there, in fact, but its tracks led farther: Ralib, the
Sleyb, made sure that the panther had struck down a
gazelle in that very place and had dragged it off. The

big cat must therefore be close by, and we had need to be doubly cautious. We scattered in the *wadi* and advanced singly.

Presently I saw, not fifty paces off, beside an overhanging bank on which the sun shone, two panther cubs at play. Round them lay the remains of their last meal—splintered bones and ragged bits of gazelle skin. Then I became aware also of the mother panther, stretched out in the shade under cover, only a part of the back and the tail showing. I motioned to Faris and Mnahi, and for a while we just watched the rare spectacle. Ralib must be somewhere near, but our eyes searched for him in vain, and of course we could not call out.

Faris lifted his rifle and communicated to me in pantomime that he meant to aim at the big panther—perhaps that her young might be taken alive. Suddenly, however, two shots came from the side, their echoes mingling in the *wadi*. The pretty game of the little robbers had come to an abrupt end; quivering and bleeding, the kittens lay on the hard gravel. Their mother, roused from her slumber, was up in a bound, flung herself over her young, snatched up one between her lips and was about to disappear from sight, when Mnahi, who until then had looked on quietly, fired. The big cat made one somersault and lay still. Sand and stones rolled down the bank. The animal did not stir; to all appearances it was dead. Now we called out and Ralib appeared with apologies; he had shot the cubs because from his position he could not see the mother.

The deadly bullet had lodged in the panther's throat. "Daughter of the Terrible One," Ralib called her. She was indeed a formidable cat. Her paws, not big but very powerful, were armed with claws as long as a man's finger, which doubtless had ripped the jugular vein of many a gazelle and antelope and broken the back of many a goat.

Ralib plunged his long knife into the panther's body, then drew it across the throat and ankles, severed the head and paws and flung them at my feet as souvenirs. Then he ripped open the belly and chest and tore out the heart. Like a savage-bred animal, he bit into the bloody tissue and sucked his mouth full of the panther's life-fluid. He believed that this potent draught would add to his own boldness and strength.

In the course of our progress Ralib discovered imprints of the big feet—the two pairs of toes—of an "Earless One," as the Bedouins call the ostrich. We followed the well-marked track until we could make out the bird with our field-glasses, far away. It was feeding. Cautiously we beat up, taking three hours to cover a couple of miles or so; then waited while the ostrich took a sandbath. Presently a second ostrich, not visible to us before, rose from the ground nearby and joined the bather—clear indication that they were brooding birds and that their nest must be quite close.

During the heat of noon the birds rested, then resumed feeding till evening. Several times they disappeared from sight, but Ralib was certain from experience that their nest was not far from the spot where the second ostrich had first shown itself; and, sure enough, before sunset the pair returned and bedded down near the place where we had first observed them.

Warily Faris, Mnahi, and I approached, following the minute instructions given us by Ralib, who remained behind with our horses. We crept up to within about fifty paces of the resting birds and took cover. With the glare gone, as the sun went down, I could easily distinguish the male from the female.

I betrayed myself by a slight movement and at once the two ostriches sprang up and ran about frantically with flapping wings. Then the hen took flight with seven bristly small chicks, the cock following protectively in the rear. The chicks, however, ran hither and thither, and Faris contrived to catch three of them and secure them by tying their legs with leather straps.

Ralib, who had come up with the mares, warned us against pursuing the ostriches. Once in full flight, they could not be overtaken by even the fleetest horse; but, if not harried, they would only run in circles and finally return to their young.

Nevertheless, Faris, caring only to bag the male, gave chase. The cock had maintained his place as rearguard, looking back frequently as he ran with paddling movements of his wings; but, when he saw the horsemen in pursuit, he abandoned his family and dashed off, now straight ahead, now zigzagging abruptly. Mnahi, Ralib, and I now joined in the chase, and in a quarter of an hour came close enough to turn the ostrich in Faris's direction. The youth threw himself from his galloping horse, which ran on a distance before it could stop. Kneeling, Faris took a hasty aim and fired twice. As the shots rang out, the bird took a tumble and remained lying on its side, fluttering. Faris leaped up, dropped rifle and cloak, and ran up to the ostrich struggling in its death throes. He whipped his knife from his belt and plunged it into the bird's throat close to the breastbone. Then he bent back the heavy wings and plucked the white display feathers, a foot long.

Ralib regarded the prey appraisingly. With his dagger he then skinned the bird, opened it, and with an expert eye carved out the best breast-pieces. Roasted, the meat tasted like that of a fat bustard and was tender enough; but to my taste the liver and the heart—the latter small for so large a bird—were better.

While we were galloping after the ostrich cock, I noticed that the hen had returned in a wide curve to the nesting-place, and at her calls the chicks came out of hiding and let themselves be herded away by her. But three of the young, those which Faris had caught and bound, could not have got away. We vainly searched for them, however, and were on the point of giving up when we discovered them, half-hidden in the sand and still as mice.

When we resumed our forward march, Faris stowed the young ostriches in the saddlebag of his own camel. Throughout the long journey he fed them on fresh buds and shoots, but particularly on caterpillars. Wild and shy at first, hunger subdued them on the second day; and before a few weeks had passed, they would trustfully feed from our hands.

☙ IX ☙

The Nufud

I HAD MY FIRST sight of the Nufud from the neighbourhood of the Shedad Umm-Kur.

And what a sight! The waves of the red desert, rising and falling evenly, seemed to extend to infinity. Crescent-shaped crests and twisted cones; a contrast of light and shade; dark red levels which rose to banks against flanks aflame with the sun. In gorges between the red walls, sixty to a hundred and sixty feet deep, a shimmer of silver and green; scattered low bushes and small trees with straight milk-white trunks and supple drooping branches bearing feathery twigs and greyish-green needles.

I held my breath, overwhelmed with amazement and admiration.

With soundless steps Maha made for the first tree, stretched her slim shapely neck and nibbled with obvious delight the yellowish young shoots and the new green needles of the *ghada*—a species of tamarisk. As far as the sand dunes of the Nufud roll, the *ghada* also is found— a boon and a blessing to camel and to man. Its roots are anchored deep in the red waste of pure quartz-sand, and it disdains other desert soil.

Maha knew the Nufud. She followed the tortuous slopes which, as in a storm-tossed ocean, led from trough to crest and, past deep chasms, to the next slope. Impossible to steer a straight course, as in the Hamad or Harra.

In endless spirals and twists we wound our way, uphill and down dale. Now and then our way led across a small level plain, but this would invariably end in a swelling dune, on the other side of which was always a bowl or a steep crater—a curious configuration, quite different from the sand dunes of the Northern Sahara with which I was familiar.

At times one would be tempted by a stretch of smooth firm ground to take a low sandy bank at a run; but Maha knew better! She knew these treacherous dunes and would not be hurried. They were really dangerous, these undulations of sand with the yielding edge that looked so harmless; and commonly there would be a steep drop into an abyss on the farther side. Sometimes we took more than half an hour to get from one dune to the next. Our small band of camel-riders had hard work to keep from being separated, but perhaps it was the herd-instinct of the camels that kept us from losing sight of each other. Faris entrusted me entirely to Maha's lead. She had spent several months each year in the Nufud and knew, it seemed to me, how to tell danger spots in advance.

This ride in the Nufud remains with me as an imperishable memory—unforgettable, that afternoon when I first beheld its brow lifted menacingly from the plain.

The fascination of the first few days made me eager to traverse the whole breadth of the red desert, though I had to own that a crossing would be exceedingly trying. From our position on the Nufud's western margin it was some three hundred miles to its eastern edge; and if in these dunes our camels made three miles or so in an hour—but not half of that, as the crow flies—they were doing well. When I expressed my wish to cross it, Faris sensibly protested that we were in no way prepared for such an undertaking and I had to content myself with Faris's extension of our ride southeast on the Nufud's margin. The desert spreads out here, sending broad tongues into the West Arabian plain; and it was over these outcrops that we first travelled, now among high dunes, then, a whole day long, across an upland flat. We rode round weathered sandstone ridges and across low depressions with dried-out rain pools, until we struck the Nufud proper again. There we reached the southernmost point of our journey. According to Faris, another day would take us to Teyma; we were thus within fifty miles of that famous oasis.

Up and down, up and down, went our way, as if over the humps of a myriad crouching, giant camels. At times our beasts became nervous and had to be led; and we even had to slip off our sandals or shoes to make headway, and on oversteep slopes stamp down footholds or shovel out steps with our hands and feet. It was fortunate that we rode *dhaluls*, accustomed from early days to the Nufud. Camels from the flint desert or the lava regions will, indeed, steadfastly refuse to set foot on these unfamiliar sands.

The cheeks of the dunes were saturated with sunshine, glowing a deeper red as the day declined. They gleamed as if they were covered with smooth crimson silk. Were these virgin dunes, never yet trodden by a human being, knowing only the innocent little feet of the dainty gazelles?

In spring the northwestern Nufud seems to abound in game. In its fastnesses breed ostriches, which later migrate with their young to the wide plains of the North, as well as gazelles and antelopes, the prey of the cruel panther. The ibex too and the eagle from the near-by Jabal Tawil, where these animals are still found, will extend their spring excursions into the red waste.

To return to our crawl over the dunes that afternoon. Something moving under some *ghadas,* far away, attracted my attention. I halted my camel and focussed my binoculars. A ravishing picture was revealed to me. A troop of snow-white Rim gazelles, with their dainty feet deep in the scarlet sand, were browsing the drooping branches in an atmosphere of silver and green. Looking more closely, I discovered other groups of gazelles near by. Some of the animals were dozing, others snuffling one another or butting each other with heads and horns. Mnahi, who had followed my example, pulled his rifle from the saddlebag; but I begged him to forbear this once and spare these beautiful animals for my sake. Mnahi saw reason. He motioned to Faris and the others, and they turned off between two dunes into a hollow, while I lingered to enjoy the sight of the charming creatures. They quench their thirst only with the dew that gathers in the morning on the leaves and flowers, say the Bedouins.

I was to have a still richer reward in that hour of silent watching. Some movements or suspicious noise must have roused the gazelles; for there they were all up on their feet, in several groups, very white on the red sand, with ears alert and all gazing toward the West. Suddenly there came over a slope, with slow, long strides, a troop of eleven ostriches—three cocks and eight hens—magnificent birds. An inquisitive gazelle-buck stole after them, but the ostriches dropped into a long trot and disappeared in the labyrinth of sand dunes.

As I rode in the wake of my comrades, a fox crossed my path, and from some acacia bushes rose many ravens. The sun was already setting and the dry air was rapidly cooling. Ahead of me the sand-waves, their crests glowing golden red, cast deep shadows towards the East. The face of the wilderness was wrapped in a violet veil. A wondrous silence rose from the Nufud. Brief dusk— then night, and a voice faintly borne to me by the wind. It was Faris looking for me. I called back; and side by side we rode into a sheltered gully surrounded by high dunes, which made an excellent camel paddock and an ideal camp site.

"Let us break our fast," said Faris, as he pulled the heavy saddle and the water-skin from the back of his *dhalul*. A fire of *ghada* sticks was soon lighted. In a few seconds this became very warm and burned without smoke and with an almost colourless flame. The men fed it with roots and sticks as thick as a man's arm. Meanwhile the bread-dough was being kneaded. As soon as there was a good heap of glowing ashes, the iron baking-sheet was placed over the fire. Together with the warm bread-cakes, the dates, honey, and hard camel-cheese tasted delicious.

Faris posted sentinels on two commanding sand-hills. One watch I had to take myself.

A clear, still night enfolded the desert. The starlight

was reflected by the dunes. The air was violet, with a silvery sheen. It was entrancing.

But the greatest wonder of all was the absolute stillness which held me entranced after I had drunk in all the beauties of the glimmering landscape and the glory of the sky, magically reflected in this unique sand-mirror. For hours I sat alone, wrapped in its mystery.

⟨⟩ X ⟨⟩

Sandstorm

WE HAD HARDLY left the Nufud, bound for the Jabal Tawil, about a hundred and fifty miles distant, when we rode into a gentle drizzle. A segment of a rainbow curved over the sand-dunes like a gleaming scimitar. Thunder rumbled from afar.

"O Thou, Almighty!" exclaimed Faris. "Blessed sound that promises us pasture!" The clouds came lower. Their grey tails swept the dune-tops. Forked lightning flashed and thunder rolled majestically, shaking the air. A fine hail rustled down. And then the clouds burst. The sand sang under the lash of the rain; the hair curled up on the drenched camels, and we riders dripped as though we had just been pulled out of water. But the deluge soon ended and a warm wind fanned us, drying man and beast. Soon the sun was out again—and by afternoon the deeper red of the dunes was the only sign that it had rained.

Two days afterwards we had descended into the stifling atmosphere of the lowlands, where the wind was driving dense dust-clouds before it.

We weathered the first day of it, though it blew with unremitting fierceness and perseverance. But on the next day it developed into a veritable sandstorm of such violence that one could barely keep one's seat in the saddle. I counselled beating back into the Nufud and there, in some low-lying depression, waiting for the storm to blow itself out. In the red sand one is quite safe. Its specific gravity is considerably greater than that of white or yellow sand, and after sufficient winter rain it is more or less covered with some vegetation.

My comrades, however, were of the opinion that the strength of the storm was already broken, that it could not possibly last longer than two days. We therefore continued our ride, hoping to see on the morrow the sun shining again on a tranquil land. But the third day was a repetition of the second, a howling gale, clouds, whirling sand, and no visibility beyond ten paces.

The heat would have been tolerable, but the air was so sultry that we dripped sweat from every pore. The perspiration could not evaporate in this muggy air, and to this discomfort was added the irritation from the driven dust. This was something new for me in Arabia. No matter how high the temperature, I had always found the air quite dry; even in winter, after rain or a thunderstorm, it will remain light and refreshing.

Half-suffocated by day, by night we were chilled to the bone by icy blasts that searched our moist bodies, and made them shake with ague.

Our hands and faces were chapped. Even our tongues ached, though we had plenty of water. The fine, white sand penetrated everywhere—under the clothes, into nose, ears, and eyes, and covering the hair. Our lips became parched; the eyes, the throat, the palate hot with inflammation and pain; the breath came in pants, the blood hammered heavily in the heart and in the temples.

Our camels dragged themselves along only with the utmost effort, groaning and complaining. In one of the saddlebags we carried one of our slaves, who had collapsed from exhaustion on the second day.

Faris had his fill of trouble with his young ostriches and their feeding. But in spite of the storm, he contrived to forage for them and always produced something—caterpillars, beetles, fresh grass and shoots, a lizard, bustard eggs. Several times a day he would direct a few spurts of milk from his *dhalul* (which had calved, as I mentioned) into the gaping mouths of the chicks. But for all his pains, the storm cost him the life of one of them.

On the third day of the storm, Faris fell ill. It was a sudden attack: first vomiting, followed by chills and fever. I kept constantly by his side, but he became alarmingly weak, until finally we had to arrange a saddlebag as a litter to carry him.

At night the storm abated somewhat, but there was no sign of a star. It was very dark and cold, and fine sand continued to blow.

On the fourth day the storm took on fresh fury. The wind howled more fiercely than ever. Our lungs were choked with dust. Worn out by the constant buffeting and sleepless nights, with aching joints, dead-tired, at the end of our strength, we groped our way forward. Two camels dropped and had to be abandoned. Their riders and loads had to be distributed among the other exhausted animals.

The worst of it was that Faris had become delirious. In the saddlebag of another camel, Dhadan, the slave who had fallen sick two days before, lay in a stupor, looking more dead than alive.

At last a vague something loomed through the driving sulphur-coloured sand-clouds; its outline grew less blurred and assumed a comforting solid shape. It was a rocky ridge, a harbour of refuge. Camels and horses crowded close against one another, while above us screamed the storm, driving before it the sand, across the top of the sheltering wall. Exhausted, men and beasts sank to the ground.

Faris, lying on rugs, had fallen into a deep coma-like slumber. I tried to cool his burning forehead and forced a little water between his parched lips. After a couple of hours or so he awoke, looking better, and gave some signs of returning strength. All the others lay on their sheepskins like men struck down, sleeping the sleep of the dead. At length I, too, propped against Maha, was overcome by sleep.

In the night I awoke, and my first thought was that I must be dreaming. A serene, starry sky looked down on a solitude sunk in deep calm. I threw off the warm fur coat which had been my coverlet and got up to look after my patient. As I bent over Faris, he opened his eyes and spoke to me. Thank Heaven, he was better and his brain was quite clear again. Hunger and thirst were his worst complaints now, and I had everything at hand to satisfy his needs. When I had also ministered to Dhadan, who had likewise improved and was able to take some stimulant, I rolled myself up once more in my fur, and instantly dropped back into deep sleep.

Daybreak found me half-awake and vaguely aware of it, through eyes still closed; but to my annoyance, Maha began to nuzzle me persistently. As I had not the least desire to get up, I pushed her head away; but she continued to prod me and to whimper softly but meaningly, until I had to open my eyes. They fell on a scene transformed. The camels were all ready and saddled; Faris—I could hardly believe my eyes—was feeding his ostrich chicks, Dhadan was watering the horses, and Mnahi was moving down the rows of camels, carrying his cloak formed into a sack and scattering from it fresh shoots he had gathered for the *dhaluls*. By the "coffee-fire" squatted Ralib, brewing the bitter essence, the enticing aroma of which scented the air.

And the sun, the wonderful sun, shone again on a world renewed; even the farthest distances were visible through the crystal-clear air, scoured by the four-days' storm.

⚙ XI ⚙

Days of Ease

O̶UR NEXT OBJECTIVE lay before us—the dark sandstone walls of the Jabal Tawil—"the long-drawn-
out Mountain." From its foot it is only an eight-hours'
ride by camel to the oasis of Jauf at the southern end of
the Wadi Sirhan. We shaped our course towards the
middle of the slope, passing over steep spurs hemmed in
by black rocks. Among the deep clefts of the ancient
range Faris knew how to pick out the one that gives
access to the Mustanda Pass, over which we could de-
scend into the plain beyond. There we found a small
Ruala camp, where we were received with open arms,
and where we decided to linger for a whole week, to rest
and pasture our *dhaluls*.

It was in this week that Faris secured the silver ankle-
rings that he had promised to his betrothed. He rode to
Jauf and there bartered one of his young ostriches for
the trinkets.

For me it was a memorable week of meditation and reflection, with no lack of new impressions. With Mnahi
I roamed the fastnesses of the Tawil; I, just for the mere
enjoyment of being there; he, on the lookout for game.
He shot a number of ibex, among them some magnificent specimens. But despite the presence of these wild
goats, the range is oppressively desolate, its predominant
tint dark, even blackish, and the outcrop of red and

slate-blue rocks seemed to deepen rather than to relieve its sombreness.

One morning I let Mnahi go on his shooting alone and instead attached myself to a herder. The camels in his charge were grazing a good way off and he came to camp only once every three days.

It was a stony tract, and all day long the camels roamed to and fro in search of feed among the boulders, which were sometimes as high as one's head. About noon we collected the herd and led it into the shade of some loftier rocks. There the herder and I stretched ourselves full length on the ground, and in lazy contentment, half asleep, we passed the warmest hours. But when the sky was clouded over, we had to keep on the move to avoid getting chilly, halting only shortly before the sun went down to draw milk for our supper into a wooden bowl.

The plants among the rocks were in bloom, with fragrant white, violet, and red flowers. Some of them imparted to the milk of our camels a peculiar but very delightful flavour, reminiscent of sweet sage or camomile or some aromatic herb. It had not the bitter taste of the milk produced in some regions, nor the watery, salty "variety" of the Wadi Sirhan. Even the camel-thorn bursts into bloom here at the base of the Jabal Tawil, and the stunted acacias shed a sweet fragrance. At times our small herd was powdered all over with pollen of a blue and yellow tint.

My herder companion was a bright, merry lad. Instead of sitting on his camel in normal fashion, he had the knack of sprawling for hours on end behind its hump, hanging on like a leech. I tried to imitate him, but it took me more than two days to learn the knack of it—how to anchor your knees in the camel's hip-bones and then, by sprawling forward and using the woolly hump of the beast as a cushion for your stomach, to ride in amazing comfort. We guided the animals with our camel-sticks, tapping them lightly, now on one shoulder, now on the other. Thus we drifted slowly along, side by side, the animals feeding as they went and halting only occasionally; but we had to keep an ever-watchful eye on our troop of camels, which were always up to some trick or other.

In those three days I learnt much. I learnt to appreciate in all their significance the noises peculiar to a camel; to realise that in the loud diapason of its stomach rumblings and in the gurglings of its throat there lies a meaning too deep for words. Even its full-throated belching is an expression of its lordly thoughts. I learnt how to deal with the sharp thorns that pierce through leather footwear, and how to treat the sting of a bee which caused the camel's lip to swell to an enormous size. My companion also taught me how to plug the udder of a mother camel, to prevent dripping and the consequent loss of precious milk, and how the baby camel could be prevented from "drinking out of hours" from the mother's udder by means of a wooden peg, fastened to its nose. I learnt to tell from the tracks on the hard gravel soil whether the camels which had passed were saddle or pack animals, and I was taught the lore of age, sex, breed and many other mysteries.

I listened with bated breath as my companions explained to me that a blue bead tied to the hairy withers of a camel was a most effective charm against the evil eye. I was told of the great ticks, as large as stag beetles, found in the camel's pelt, and of the lovely blue-black crows which hop about undisturbed on its back, helping themselves with prying beaks to these ticks and other parasites, which lie snugly in the thick, matted hair.

The delight of watching the little baby camels made my three days of wandering worth while. What quaint, lovable creatures they are! How they enjoy licking and smelling each other! They sprawl awkwardly on their overlong legs in groups of five or six, and rub their long, slim necks against some strange mother, making her happy in the delusion that she has brought into the world such a large brood of dear, ridiculous creatures.

When the warm rain fell on the coats of the camels, large or small, they developed "marcel" waves, curls, and fringes, which would have delighted a fashionable ladies' *coiffeur*.

And when we sat down before a fire, with our backs to the rocks, and my companion chattered away, telling me story after story, it was amusing to see how the camels would press close up, and listen intently, as if they understood him. True, now and again, they would interrupt the story with a hearty belch and go on placidly chewing the cud of flowery herbage and thistle-fodder, to the accompaniment of a loud and discordant grinding of teeth. But that is the way of camels.

Every morning I awoke to see the sun rising or just risen through a perfect forest of legs, for all the world like stilts, or under an archway of long necks.

◈ XII ◈

Camels, Women, Children— and Locusts

OH, THESE CAMELS! They stamp and trample; they buck, they quarrel, they weep and take fright— yes! And they laugh; they are helpless, but ever and anon rebellious. They will run like a machine for hours, and all at once stop or refuse to budge. Only with a rider in the saddle are they erect, proud animals, self-assured, noble, moving with elastic strides. With a dull herdsman seated on its hump, a camel too becomes dull, lazy and—gluttonous.

The camel is not merely a creature to ride. The nomad makes use of it in many other ways. He cooks its wiry sinews and leathery muscles and eats them, though, even after boiling, the flesh is so tough that one's teeth are either blunted or loosened in the effort to chew it. The Arab drinks the camel's milk, and often in times of stress he will drink the turbid, sour fluid secreted in the creature's stomach. On cold mornings the people warm their hands in the camel's urine and even wash their hair with it. It works deadly destruction on the parasites! The wool of the camel is collected and woven into material for herdsmen's coats and for the garments of the women and children. The poor animals are loaded with incredible burdens; their dung provides fuel for fires and their hides are cut up for water-bags, belts, and sandals.

In the grey of one morning I noticed a woman moving amongst the resting animals. Whenever she saw a female camel get up, she would hurry and catch the urine, for which she was waiting, in a bowl she carried for the purpose. The camel's urine smells sweetly of herbs and aromatic plants, it must be remembered. Returning to her tent, one side of which was open, I saw her gather the loose tresses of her little daughter's hair in her hand and dip them into this much-prized hair-wash. She then combed, parted and braided the damp black hair into the usual lovelocks. Again I saw her return to the camels; but suddenly she sat down. A moment later she rose again, threw away her bowl, and hurried back toward her tent, but collapsed before she had gone far. I sprang up and ran to her.

She said never a word as I tried to help her to her feet; she only withdrew her arms from my hold and cowered on the ground. Then I noticed that she was in labour. As there was no adult within hearing, I called to the woman's little girls to bring bedding and sheepskins. With these I made a couch for her, right among the camels, sent the children back to the tent, and planted myself as a screen before the woman with a sheepskin held over her. Thus she gave birth to her first son.

Presently her husband arrived and two slaves of Faris's. The father picked up the newly born babe, and the three men ran to a camel, kicked it in the hip to make it rise, and with their right hands continued to massage the beast's right flank until it let down urine. With this they bathed the squealing, downy infant all over, baptizing him with this herb-scented water of the beast of the desert into the sacred fellowship of the wilderness.

I was still thinking how unexpectedly this incident had come to pass, when I was startled by heavy pattering on the tent-roof and on the sand outside. Everywhere, on tents and on the backs of the camels, it was raining big, fat, reddish locusts!

The new baby boy's mother was just then squatting in her smoke-filled tent, engaged, with the assistance of her women friends, in swathing his little body in a plaster of dried camel dung and old rags—a measure considered indispensable among the Bedouins for the protection of newly born children. But, all-important as this ceremony was, all the women except the mother rushed away pell-mell, to help their menfolk and children to harvest the locusts.

These kept coming up in swarms—nay, in cloud piled on cloud. While myriads whirred past and on with a loud noise, a host of them broke flight and settled. Wherever one looked, the ground was thick with them, covered, as it were, with a crawling red carpet. Grass, herbage, bushes melted away under the devouring mass of insects. And the whole camp was out gathering them.

Soon locusts were roasting at every fire, round which men, women, and children squatted in a circle. They picked up the insects by their gauzy wings, plucked off the legs, dipped the roasted "husks" in salt, and ate them, skin and all.

Boiled, I did not like locusts; they had the taste of particularly insipid cabbage or some such vegetable.

Roasted, I found them more palatable; crisp outside, and inside something like tender spinach. In neither case did they taste at all like meat. They are clean animals and as food not at all unpleasant, but one soon gets very tired of them, when one has to eat nothing else day after day.

All round the camp and all day long smoke screens were kept going, into which women and children drove the locusts. Next morning mountains of these insects lay drying in the sun, and when we left this camp site a few days later, there was not an empty sack or saddle-bag, and our camels carried gigantic loads of the dried insects. Men and women, dogs and camels, fed on them —but only for a few days; after that, they turned one's stomach. But what was left was carefully preserved for other and leaner times, for when the locusts swarm in vast numbers, one can safely predict drought and famine.

As we followed in the wake of these marauders, we found the land stripped bare; every bit of herbage had disappeared under their greedy maws. But I came to realize that the "plague of locusts" is not so utterly devastating in the desert as it is to the tillers of the soil in Transjordania, Palestine, and Egypt. In the desert it is a great blessing for all creatures. Buzzards, ravens, bustards and other desert game-birds fattened on the locusts, and flocks of storks trailed after the red clouds. Even to the human desert-dwellers they may be most useful. Faris told me that tens of thousands of Bedouins had to subsist for weeks on locusts alone, and that at times their camels and horses too can have no other fodder. During four-days' march northward—forty-five

to fifty miles from our last camp by the Jabal Tawil—
we found all the pasture gone, consumed to the last
blade by the locusts. It was only in the plain of Biyaz
that we found a depression which was untouched and
with plenty of forage. There we made camp under the
shelter of a *wadi*.

The women and slaves unloaded the camels and at
once proceeded to put up the tents. The tent-cloth is
spread on the ground, looking like a long, black, hairy
hide; the lines are drawn east and west, tent-pegs driven
home with wooden mallets, and the long tent-poles,
properly spaced, are inserted under the roof-strip. Then,
by dint of lifting and pushing, up goes the structure;
first one pole in place, then the next, and so on until the
whole goat-hair "house" rests securely on its supports.
Row after row of tents rose, casting long shadows as the
last sun-rays gleamed on their peaked roofs.

I bought a weakly camel from my fellow-travellers,
had it slaughtered and the meat distributed to all and
sundry. The flesh-pots of Ishmael were soon steaming
and the savour of them attracted a horde of hungry
dogs. One of the tribesmen was to play host to myself,
Faris, and a number of others. Out of the dark his troop
of camels stole up silently, showing suddenly in the light
of the fire as if they had come from nowhere, and lay
down before his tent. It was comfortable and homely
there by the fire, in the wide circle of men and beasts.

Our cook had transferred a turbid, muddy mess of
old coffee grounds and water from a goatskin bag to a
pot with a long spout, which he put on the hearth. Now
the black, bitter brew foamed up again, and after it had

been properly skimmed, the cook poured a part into the smallest jug available and from this served his coffee a few drops at a time, a single stoneware cup making the round of the company. The mound of camel dung heaped by the women was glowing red, and everyone was on the tiptoe of expectation when Faris rose and went over to the women's side of the tent. A cheerful bustling sounded from it—supper ought to be about ready; and sure enough, there appeared a woman and a slave, carrying between them a huge platter piled high with meat, which they set down on the threshold. Faris shouted into the night, to call all stragglers who might be in the vicinity.

We grouped ourselves round this mountain of flesh. I saw in the flickering light wild-looking, hungry men squatting opposite me, with black plaits of hair showing under their white-and-red head-cloths, the tips of which were flung over the shoulders. They fell to with their fingers, tore the meat from the bones and devoured it in great gulps. Our host flung titbits to me across the platter. It was embellished with the camel's head split open, but without the brains. Only the women will eat them, for they are supposed to make men faint-hearted. The hearts of bustard and other fowl are also disdained by these gallant lords of the desert.

We lingered four days in this depression, as we had enough food and fuel. The camels scattered to graze in the surrounding country. The women, too, were busily employed in hoeing up the roots of the small shrubs and gathering their twigs, which they carried to camp on their backs in large bundles. Many of the women had splendid figures, and they walked straight, with swaying hips, even under the heavy loads they carried. The long trains of their blue gowns trailed behind them on the sand, but the front was gathered high enough—but only just high enough—about a hand's breadth—to give them freedom in walking.

Eleven days of leisurely travelling brought us next to al-Khor, low-lying country pitted with rain pools, south of the Jabal Enaza. There Faris and I parted from our fellow travellers and rode westward to the boundary of the Hamad (gravel steppe) and the Harra (flint desert), making for a *wadi* in the neighbourhood of the Jabal Umm Wual. Darkness fell upon us in the lowlands, but on the higher levels of the Harra enough daylight lingered for us to see ahead. I pulled up Maha, for a fairy scene was spread out before me—the encampment of the Ruala at evening.

After seeing nothing but the empty wilderness, day after day and weeks on end—nothing but the sky and solitude—there suddenly appeared to us a city of tents! Smoke rose from thousands of black dwellings, and in between, large camel-herds, hundreds of them, were wending their way home.

At last we were at home again. Seven hundred and fifty miles in the saddle lay behind us, through the virgin desert of the Hamad and the Nufud; and I had brought back a priceless store of unforgettable memories.

⊚ XIII ⊚

Tuëma

IT WAS THE day after our return. Faris and I were lying on a hillock, idly watching his father's roaming herds. He spoke of his sweetheart with emotion and somewhat quaintly: "She who approaches in the camel-litter"—"she who is hidden behind the veils of the riding-tent"—"the guarded one"—"the strong *dhalul* shall carry her through the deep shadowy valley until the rising sun reddens her cheeks with its radiance——"

Faris was a poet, and in love.

A Bedouin maiden came riding by on a camel, driving another camel with its calf before her.

"Mawia!" cried Faris. It was a friend of Tuëma. She slid from her *dhalul* and spoke to the animals, which obediently stopped and waited.

"Where is my sister?" Faris asked.

She smiled and answered: "Tuëma hath awaited thy home-coming day by day."

Faris stood up and went close to the girl. "When thou meetest her," said he, "bid her remember those nights when she and I met in secret. Tell my beloved that I long to walk with her in the sand dunes. The trail of her gown will obliterate our footsteps, and none shall know where we abide."

"Faris!" the girl protested.

"Tell her the blade of my dagger reminds me that I

shall never be at peace until the slender blossom bends before the storm of my love," he said.

A few hours later Tuëma came. Her friend had given her the good news of her lover's return.

She appeared over the brow of a hill. Then she drew rein and leapt from her sorrel, drawing the halter between its forelegs and tying it over the left hock; thus the mare was free to graze, but could not run away.

Tuëma walked toward us with the grace of a fawn and we went to meet her. She put her arms around Faris's neck and said tenderly: "O thou, my life." And he replied: "O thou, my faith." Then we sat down together on the hill-top.

Tuëma cast her eyes about and asked with a mischievous laugh: "Where is my bunch of wild flowers? My big beautiful bouquet?"

"Thy bunch of flowers?"

"Yes, and the silver anklets?"

Faris put on an air of importance and jingled the trinkets which he had in his pocket. Tuëma then gave him a look of surprise and, jumping up, reached for the hand which he had thrust into his pocket; but with the other he held her arm fast and said: "Thou must shut thy eyes and not open them until I have kissed them."

She did as he bade her. Then he drew from his pocket the silver bangles which he had procured in Jauf and slipped them on Tuëma's ankles. She begged and begged to be allowed at least one look at the gift. "Not yet," cried Faris; "first I must deck thee with the flowers of the desert, the imperishable ones."

One by one the enamoured youth unloosed the ends

of the girl's glossy, black braids and twined into them fourteen magnificent white ostrich plumes, each a foot long. When he had done this, he drew the long tresses forward over her shoulders and gathered them into one hand, so that the shivering plumes formed a bouquet, and kissed her eyelashes. "Here, my sister," he said, "is the bouquet I promised thee, of everlasting flowers."

She opened her eyes and gazed with wonder on her lover's gift. Then she buried her face in the plumes and twined her arm about him.

Faris leaned his head on her shoulder, and placing his hand over her heart, said: "It jumps like a wild rabbit."

"It will become quite tame in thy hand," she murmured.

"Hast thou never before permitted a young man to put his hand on thy heart?" he asked.

Tuëma flushed. "No, never; only thee."

◉ XIV ◉

The Hunger March

AMIR FUAZ, who had gone to Damascus some time before, was to rejoin his migrating tribe when it had
reached the *Wudian* district of Rueyshdat. That would
be before the end of the week. I took advantage of the
brief interval to make an excursion into the Harra with
Faris and a few of his followers. I liked it no better than
did our camels, though they were fresh saddle-animals.

The Harra is a long stony desert running southeast
from the Jabal Druz (or Hauran) and borders on the
great Arabian desert-plateau. Volcanic mountains over-
look it on the northwest. It is intersected with a network
of ancient camel trails, for in the Harra the routes of
both the western and eastern Bedouin tribes cross. The
region, up to the Jabal Enaza, has the reputation of
being the coldest in North Arabia. It has a mean eleva-
tion of about three thousand feet, and for months in the
year is exposed to chill northeast gales and cold snaps,
when the thermometer will drop to six degrees below
zero, Celsius (10.8 below freezing-point, Fahrenheit).

This year, indeed, the spring was a mild one throughout the region. But the monotonous, undulating, stony
surface showed a touch of meagre vegetation only near
rain pools in low-lying places. Elsewhere it was all gleaming flat flints, polished pebbles and porous pumice. Rust-
coloured, bluish-grey, blackish and speckled splinters
covered the floor of the Harra as with a coat of scales,

one or two layers deep. If you raked them away, you found underneath yellowish and reddish sand inter-mingled with flints. Under the glare of the sun, the ground glittered unbearably, so that one could not look at it long without causing the eyes to smart. There was a steady crunching and clattering as we rode over the stony field, which made very difficult going for our camels. The leathery hoof-pads slipped on the polished stones and they often lost their footing. This unfriendly desert did not please me at all. I must admit, however, that the air was pure and bracing.

When we reached Rueyshdat on the day agreed, Fuaz was already there, back from Damascus; and there also was gathered most of his tribe, for the region of Rueysh-dat seemed to be the only one in Northern Arabia where enough rain-water could be found this spring.

Here the Ruala were watering their camels, probably for the last time before they reached the wells of Abu Rijmeyn, two hundred and sixty miles away. A forced march—a gamble with life and death as the stakes—confronted the whole of the Ruala tribe. They could not go back, neither into the Wadi Sirhan nor into the Jauf Basin. They must go forward, right through enemy territory, under the threat of skirmishes, perhaps real war, with hostile Bedouin tribes. But far more dangerous appeared to the Ruala the contest with Nature. Scanty pasture still clothed the stony uplands and hills; the stems of the tiny plants still held a sprinkling of sap, so that the camels could still find a little nourishment and moisture. Perhaps also God the Merciful would show in-dulgence to the Ruala and on their march into the

North send them the longed-for rains. There had been no rain for weeks, except only in the region of Rueysh-dat, where it had rained almost in torrents. The broad depressions were still full of water and smaller pools and puddles were dotted all over the district.

At last came the time for the start. The whole desert basin was alive and thronging with herds moving in one great heaving mass. There arose the confused din of more than three hundred thousand animals, which for miles round spread a penetrating musk-like smell.

Apart, on the flanks of the main mass, were the pack-camels, laden with tents, equipment, provisions, and so forth, under the guard of their drivers. Hundreds of lofty travelling-litters loomed up among them—the *kethabs* of the *shiyukhs* and wealthy tribesmen, tall "riding-tents" with widely curved horns, balanced on the backs of the long-legged beasts. Their interiors are adorned with costly silk and cashmere stuffs; the seats and backs are lined with rugs and padded with soft cushions. Like the wings of giant butterflies, the spreading sides of these tall and airy structures dipped above the tossing sea of animals.

Unceasingly, the stream of camels welled up from the basin to unite in an immense tidal wave more than five miles wide. The great columns of the camel trains began to take shape. With tireless energy, in all this heat, dust and noise, riders on sweating horses galloped from side to side, directing the herders where to fall in with their charges, mother camels and baby camels. The air resounded with the roaring, braying and squealing of the camels, the neighings of horses, the calls and curses of the herders, the shrieking of women and the whining of children. Scattered here and there among the ever-widening lines of advancing camels rode armed men, convoying their families. Thus out of apparent chaos arose the disciplined order of a general tribal migration, pushing forward into the uncertain wilderness.

As Amir Fuaz rode forward with me, past the marching columns, we were greeted from all sides. Tribesmen trotted across to cry hail and good fortune to their war lord. Slaves dismounted and kissed his feet or pressed their faces against them with a blessing. Women and girls shouted shrilly their "Zaraghrit!" or cried ecstatically: "Allah strengthen thee! Go thou before the countenance of our Lord! Ya el-'Adi—O dispenser of bounty. Long life to thee, our Prince! God grant thy wishes!"

⚗ XV ⚗

Famine and War

TARFA, SISTER OF Amir Fuaz, who had married Mij-hem ibn Meheyd, the Chief of the Fid'an, died sud-denly. Thereupon, what must the fifty-five-year-old widower do but forthwith sue for the hand of another sister of the Ruala Prince, Fuwasa, who was seventeen. Fuaz refused, and declared publicly, before the men in assembly, that he considered Ibn Meheyd too old for his young sister. Thereupon the vain Fid'an chief flew into a towering rage and swore that he would take venge-ance, not only on his brother-in-law, Amir Fuaz, but also on the whole Ruala tribe, and the Sha'lan family in particular. All this ultimately came to pass.

During the last few months, Ibn Meheyd had matured his plans for revenge. He had stirred up the neighbour-ing tribes of the Fid'an into joining him in war on the Ruala. It seemed as if the famine, threatened by the failure of rain in the Hamad and other grazing regions, would now become an additional formidable ally of Amir Fuaz's foes. Thirty-five thousand Ruala, with seven thousand tents and about three hundred and fifty thousand camels would be forced to invade the grazing territory of enemies, unless sufficient rain fell in the Hamad within the next few days.

As yet, life ran its familiar round. But over all hov-ered the spectres of thirst, hunger, and death.

The Ruala did not fear war. Were they not strong

and undefeated for one hundred and thirty-seven years? As yet, they had no suspicion of Ibn Meheyd's activities, but he had, to all intents and purposes, united eight other tribes with his Fid'an. They only lacked a suitable pretext. Nature, however, helped them meanwhile by wearing out the powerful and high-spirited Ruala.

Hot winds swept over the Hamad and the Syrian steppe—but never a drop of rain. Unusual heat brooded over North Arabia, so that everything withered. The Ruala pushed onwards faster and faster and lengthened the day's marches. From one horizon to the other the vast herds covered the wilderness. It was almost as if the herders had lost all control over the starving and thirsty animals. Every morning, like clouds of locusts, the camels overflowed the desert on a front of fifteen to over twenty miles. Small, shrivelled herbs were their only nourishment and the small amount of moisture in the plants was all that saved them from dying of thirst.

There was something gigantic and exalting in this un-exampled struggle of man and beast for very existence against the pitiless forces of Nature. Those who were unequal to the struggle quietly succumbed. The count-less herds moved slowly over the boundless plains, which here and there still showed faint touches of forage, more grey than green. To my amazement, I discovered that the fat, brick-red hairy caterpillars which, in spite of the drought, were to be found on every stalk and flower, not only helped to nourish hundreds of thousands of desert fowl, bustards, and gazelles, but also our camels and horses. Troops of gazelles were in flight from death in the wilderness, striving with a last effort to reach the distant Euphrates. It was as if a tremendous fire were sweeping up from the heart of Arabia, and man and beast were in headlong flight to escape from its consuming breath.

The eternal law of Nature was being fulfilled: death to the weak, the maimed, and the forsaken. The strong trampled over the weak, gaining from their victims fresh strength and endurance to push on. Though famine ravaged the land, the slaves in the camp of the nomad chieftain saw to it that the guests of their master lacked nothing. Every day for breakfast I was served a dish very like our scrambled eggs, made of several tiny eggs of the sand grouse. It had a particular gamy tang, and so has a similar dish made of the much larger bustard eggs. Fresh truffles were roasted in the embers of weeds and camel dung, their rinds splitting in the heat. Every morning I found beside my bowl of milk a basin of wild honey, with thick dabs of sheep's-milk butter floating in it. As I was eating, I watched the slave baking bread. He poured a porridge-like mixture of wheat flour, crushed seeds and herbs on to a hot, convex iron plate, resting on three stones over the fire. The batter first spread out on this grid, and then wrinkled up under the heat and formed large griddle cakes, brown and thick, which, one by one, the Negro peeled off and threw into our laps. We tore off strips from these wafer-like, charcoal flakes, crisp at the edges, rolled them around our fingers, and with these morsels fished the butter out of the honey. We strangers and guests certainly did not suffer want. Most of the Rualas, on the contrary, and even the chieftains, actually went hungry.

It was touching to see a tribesman, himself half-starved, bring to his *sheykh's* tent a hare or a gazelle, or other game, as an offering for the sustenance of his chieftain's guests. Even children and women came by every day, and from a clothes-bundle laid down a handful of truffles or a wild pigeon. Once a boy brought me a large, fat lizard which he had killed with a stone, and later a rock-badger and a yellow-headed vulture. The boy asked if, in such time of famine, he might presume to offer me such animals for food.

". . . and so it was when Israel had sown, that the Midianites came up, and the Amalekites and the children of the East, even they came up against them, and they encamped against them and destroyed the increase of the earth . . . *for they came up with their cattle and their tents, and they came as grasshoppers for multitude; for both they and their camels were without numbers. . . .*" (Judges vi, 3–5.)

With gnawing stomachs and with drooping spirits, the Ruala followed their dying herds. Ever farther northwards they pressed on, close to the enemies' territory. Every day hundreds of camels and also many people fell by the wayside, while the survivors strained all the more desperately to reach the hills of Abu Rijmeyn. The weaker remained where they fell. The moment a camel, at the end of its strength, commenced to stagger and threatened to fall, riders in the neighbourhood leapt from their mounts and, dashing up to the poor creature, put it out of its misery. Meanwhile the others marched

on unconcerned, without a check. The man remaining
behind would cut up the camel in a few minutes, then
hurry on to catch up with the tribe, leaving only the
entrails, the head and legs, on the trampled ground.

The losses in the camel herds increased day by day.
From some hundreds a day they had risen to sinister figures. According to Fuaz, two thousand camels died or
had to be killed daily.

Onward, ever onward; though hostile tribes made
some attempt to stem this tide of hungry men and
beasts, and the Saba and the Fid'an drove off a few of
the smaller herds, the main body of the Ruala was as yet
safe from attack. But isolated skirmishes and small raids
grew in number the farther the Ruala drew away from
the independent domain of Ibn Sa'ûd, and passing
through Transjordania, penetrated into Syria. There indeed the situation threatened to become serious. French
aeroplanes droned over the restless sea of men and beasts,
but so far only scouting planes were out, seeking to
ascertain the strength of the invading Ruala host.

The "Fransawi" could not, without some protest, permit a whole nation of warlike Bedouins to roam so far
beyond its own ground and invade Syria. The settlers in
the French mandated territory were already shaking for
fear of war among the Bedouin tribes, and were making
preparations for the defence of their villages and fields.
The Druses, on the contrary, warlike people of the
Hauran Mountains, were perhaps rejoicing in anticipation of a new turmoil in Syria, from which they might
hope to gain more than they had from the last. In that
quarrel the Ruala, hereditary enemies of the Druses, did

not take sides against the French. The French authorities immediately realized the danger, and promptly gave orders that the ancient caravan route from Damascus to Tudmur (Palmyra) and Deyr-ez-Zor (which passes south of the hills of the Abu Rijmeyn and branches off near Tudmur towards Baghdad) was to form the most northerly boundary beyond which the Ruala might not seek pasture. None must cross this line if armed or mounted.

Now the foes of the Ruala could triumph!

The Saba, the Muwali, Hadediyyin and all the others had the law of the land and the power of the French Government on their side—and they were confederates of Ibn Meheyd! What did they care for the misery of the Ruala? They only saw at hand a long-desired opportunity to fall upon and destroy this hated Ruala nation and take possession of their vast herds.

It was a day in April, when our distress seemed to have reached the last extremity beyond which endurance could not go—when death stared every man and animal in the face—that I entered the tent of Faris, which was pitched on a hillock a little apart. The tent was empty. The mother and sister of the young man were probably searching for truffles, roots and dry herbs for fuel. As I flung myself down by the glowing ashes inside the tent, I heard the voice of Faris ibn Naif behind the tent. It was loud and excited, which was an unusual thing for him, for the calm and self-control of my friend had always been exemplary. He was neither a Philistine nor a bigot, but a man of a moral purity such as I never found surpassed, even among the Bedouins. I wondered, therefore, that I should now hear Faris so excitedly wrangling with someone. But when I stepped round the tent and saw him, I was undeceived. He stood with clenched fists, his face raised to the sky, in an attitude of supplication. He obviously believed himself secure from human observation, and it was obvious also that he conversed with no human being.

He spoke to God, and his prayer was an expression of the anguish of his soul.

"Thou art merciful," I heard him cry. "Thou seest that our suffering and our dying have become cruel. We are starving to death. The helpless have no hope except in Thee. . . ."

Faris was a Muslim in name only. He cried out like a child to his Father. He implored—and raged in turn. He stamped his feet and clenched his fists in impotent fury. He bowed his head in humility—he raised his eyes in anger, but he also wept bitterly. He stretched out his empty hands, crying: "O Lord, the people perish, men and beasts starve, give pasture—give water—give bread —give peace. . . ."

Without letting him see me, I slipped back to his tent. I sat down by the hearth and poked with the fire-irons in the glowing dung, and held out my hands over it. Involuntarily I folded them and thought of the childlike faith of Faris, and I too begged God for aid. "Thou must help—the need is great; the herds are starving and the nation is dying."

When I raised my eyes, Faris stood before me. "Thou art sad, my Brother?" he asked affectionately.

I rose and grasped his proffered hand. "No," I said.

"No longer sad, for Allah will no longer shut us out from the blessings of His heaven."

At this moment we saw Amir Fuaz with his mounted bodyguard ride past. They saw us also and came over and sat down in the tent.

In the course of the conversation, Faris said to the young Amir: "Let Aziz and me travel to thy enemies and treat with them. If they give in and share their pastureland with us, the French will then make no objections."

With some anger the young Amir fixed his eyes on Faris and cried: "We shall act, but no longer treat with them. We shall take what we want of our enemy's pasturage. Without forage there can be no camels, and without camels no life for us. Hast thou not perceived that?"

"I understand," said Faris, in his gentle way. "Is it then no longer a custom with us that one may beg his life, even of the enemy when compelled by need? Truly the path of peace is shorter than the long road on which lurks destruction."

Fuaz did not answer—and all the others in the tent held their peace. Suddenly, however, the young Prince got up, strode over to the slave who was watering his mare from a goatskin, mounted and rode away.

◈ XVI ◈

A New Lease of Life

A NEW DEVELOPMENT BROUGHT a glint of hope that extreme measures might be avoided. A message arrived from the Commandant at Rutbah, in British territory, Muhammed Yassin Bey, inviting Amir Fuaz to a conference in that town; he, Yassin Bey, was ready to treat with the Head of the Ruala concerning their admission to pastures and wells in Iraq.

Fuaz decided to accept the invitation. If he could reach an agreement with Yassin Bey, and this was approved by the British authorities—who otherwise must disavow their own official—it would mean that the whole tribe could pass the summer securely near the Euphrates. So he would go to Rutbah. It would be a last attempt to save his people from their desperate plight by peaceable means.

Further news, however, clouded this prospect. An emissary, actually a spy, of the Ruala returned to our camp with the intelligence that Yassin Bey meant treachery, that his invitation was a trap; once in Rutbah Amir Fuaz would be taken prisoner or quietly assassinated. This account was confirmed by a letter from a devoted confidant of the Ruala in Rutbah, who was a soldier in the Camel Corps there. He claimed to possess knowledge of secret instructions issued by the Commandant, and his statements generally squared with the spy's. I could not, however, quite believe it. That Yassin Bey, considering his position, should contemplate such action seemed to me on the face of it unlikely, and the show of evidence was not good enough; it was too much like rumour.

The matter was discussed at length in council. The Amir's half-brother, Mijhem, expressed his conviction that there was grave danger of a trap, and urged the utmost wariness. His plan was that Fuaz should set out with a single chosen attendant skilled in spying, and stop a safe distance this side of Rutbah. There Fuaz should keep in hiding while his companion made his way unobtrusively into the fortress in order to ascertain the truth of the situation. My advice was different. I suggested to Fuaz that he should leave Rutbah severely alone and go right on to Baghdad, to negotiate with the British high authorities directly. Mijhem spoke against my counsel, and Amir Fuaz rejected it.

The upshot of it all was the adoption of Mijhem's plan. Fuaz started by motor-car for Rutbah immediately after the council, taking with him Mijhem himself. For the time of his absence, the Amir transferred the command of the tribe to his uncle, Tra'd ibn Sattam. The same day word came from our rear that the tail of the Ruala had also crossed the border, so that the whole nomad nation was now in Syria.

Every day the whole tribe must shift camp. When I got up at the first rays of the sun, this was already in progress. The camel-herd was gone from my tent row. The spacious abodes of our temporary leader, Tra'd ibn Sattam, and his three sons had been taken down, slaves were rolling up the tenting and covering the remains of the fire with sand. Milk-white camels were brought up for the women and girls of the *Sheykh's* household and made to kneel, so that they could mount to the travelling-litters on their backs.

In litters and saddlebags were carried the young of all species. From the lofty "riding-tent" of a *sheykh* looked out a smiling woman with a child at her breast. A camel calf, too unsteady as yet to travel on its feet, hung in a hamper suspended from its mother's hump; on her other side the wistful faces of two little girls peeped from the saddlebag. A troop of baby camels a few days old crowded up curiously and their mothers came and nuzzled them and tried to push them away.

Carried on camels in special saddle-frames, or hanging limply in the arms of their riders, were young foals, exhausted and starved, because the mother mares had been dry for days. Only the dogs were fat. They could glut themselves on the droves of fallen animals.

The multitude of the assembled tribe, with its chattels and herds, had swelled to gigantic proportions. Nothing like it had happened for generations. The whole nation was in movement. This was not one of the ordinary migrations that take place in the spring or autumn; rather was it one of the historic tribal exoduses that occur once in a generation—or century.

In their hundreds of thousands, grunting camels swarmed over the face of the wilderness. Their long necks rose and fell rhythmically. They undulated and flowed on as if they were carried forward by some invisible movement of the ground. Like locusts, they looted the scanty greyish-green pasture before their hungry mouths. Not a trace of vegetation survived their passage. They left behind nothing but naked, trampled earth, and over it a veil of dust and mist that hung in the still air for hours.

At the head of the advancing nation, in front of the centre of the first line, strode one fawn-colored camel, bearing on its back a singular structure adorned with hundreds of small tufts of black ostrich feathers and barbaric decorations. The large framework of acacia wood was balanced and secured on a saddle of special design. It was the *Markab*, the "Ship", also called *Abu-Duhur*, "Father of the Ages"—the Ark of Ishmael. It is the altar before which Bedouins for centuries have made their votive and thank-offerings. There is only one such Ark in all Arabia. For ages past it has moved from tribe to tribe, as one conquered the other. The Ruala had held it now for nearly one hundred and fifty years, and to them it has become the symbol of their unity and their emblem of war,—the tribal Great Banner, as it were. This ancient and hallowed standard, the Ruala will tell you, has been moved by the spirit of Allah at critical periods in their history, especially in grave and decisive conflicts, to reveal to them when and where to face the enemy and join battle.

This day, too, they expected to see God's presence and protection revealing themselves in mystic signs from the old frame on the camel's back.

⊛ XVII ⊛

The War Goddess

TRA'D IBN SATTAM hurried with me to the sacred Standard, which rose high above the travelling-litters. We made our way through an agitated throng. The buzz of women's and children's voices intermingled with the grunting and complaining of laden camels. On nearer approach I noticed a group of women afoot, threading their way to the Standard; they waved their head-cloths and kept up a high-pitched chant. They were escorting a young woman, walking sedately in their midst. It was Tuëma. Her beautiful serene face was radiant and aglow with health. Her eyes under their long lashes were grave and devout, but she had a bright glance for Tra'd ibn Sattam, who had chosen her out of all the Ruala maidens for the signal honour of riding in the *Markab,* and on recognizing me her cheeks dimpled with a smile.

When Tuëma and her train of women had come up with the camel which bore the tribal symbol, a tall powerful animal led by a slave, she ran by its side for a space. The trilling and waving of the women rose to a joyous frenzy. Suddenly Tuëma broke away from her retinue, and with a running start grasped the camel's shoulder-girth and climbed nimbly on to its back and into the Palladium. In the left fore-corner of the sacred structure was a seat with a footrest, and on this she composed herself, enthroned on high like a desert queen above her people. Thereupon, she untied her head-cloth and her glorious tresses fell over her shoulders. At a sign from her, the escorting women, who had continued to walk beside the camels, climbed up again to their several litters.

From the midst of the migrating multitude now came the sounds of shots fired in jubilation, and soon tribesmen were galloping forward from all directions. They assembled and in a body raced toward the *Markab*, Faris at their head. Amidst the thunder of hoofs and the glint of carbines, there arose the wild chant of the young men as they pressed around their queen.

Tuëma had risen and stood erect in the lofty frame. Her face became transfigured in an ecstasy of joy. Suddenly she put both her hands to her throat and tore open her dress and broke into jubilant song. With bared breast she rose, straining her supple body until she was poised high above the ark, holding aloft a bunch of snow-white ostrich plumes. She looked like a goddess— the bravest and most beautiful maiden of her great tribe. She cried to the youths words of passionate eloquence. She inflamed them with warlike ardour. She exhorted them to remember the heroes who once had chained themselves to this Standard by means of the iron shackles of their mares, so that they might not leave their queen, but defend her to the last breath.

Faris's eyes were fixed in rapture on Tuëma, on her lofty throne. In his hand flashed the sword of Jidua, a great hero of the Ruala. He carried the historic blade to his lips with both hands and kissed it. "O Tuëma, guardian of my soul!" he cried. Then he wheeled his horse and raced off with his riders.

Tra'd ibn Sattam took the leading rope of Tuëma's camel from the slave and led her past the marching tribe. For all the dire distress, a festive spirit animated the whole people. It was a festal day, for the Ruala had a queen again—a virgin in the sacred Ark; and under her symbolic leadership they pressed forward to their destiny.

Evening came and the whole tribe made camp. But in the grey of the next dawn they were on the march again.

Armed motor-cars circled about the widespread herds and guarded the flanks of the great migration. Despite the fact that we marched in close formation, it was inevitable under the conditions that single families or even groups of them, with their camels, should lag behind or struggle in detachments; these would be an easy prey for the enemy, of whose presence we were fully aware from the surprise attacks made each day by strong mounted bands and the appearance of numerous hostile fighting-motors.

☙ XVIII ☙

The Land of Promise

EVERY EVENING THE Ruala occupied new pastures—
such as they were—farther north. The drought in
each camp was terrible. Long since I had given up the
luxury of wiping my face in the morning with a mois-
tened face-rag. In the Amir's household Mnahi was
charged with rationing the water supply. He knew
nothing of liquid measures, but he soon devised one for
his purpose. He put a pebble, which he always kept
handy, into a small wooden bowl and, for each of us
tent-mates, poured over it just enough water to cover
it. It was precious little.

As with the water, so with the milk. Camels which,
on good pasture, used to give between four and five
quarts of milk a day, now gave less than one. To save
this little for themselves and their horses, the Ruala had
to kill the new-born camel calves. The herds were a
sorry sight—emaciated, jaded, covered with dust.

I was talking with the *shiyukhs* about certain grazing
lands northeast of us when Faris, who had overheard our
conversation, said to me: "Let us go and explore Abu
Rijmeyn and the farther hills and take a look at the
pasture, so as to reassure our people." We decided then
and there to journey into that promising, but forbidden,
land.

This reconnaissance, which we made by motor—Faris,

I, and two slaves—had consequences which we did not then anticipate.

We held a straight northerly course until we crossed the old Tudmur-Baghdad caravan route—"The Road of Death", as the Ruala had come to call it since the French Administration had forbidden them to cross it. Their camps were already within thirty-odd miles of it.

The scenery changed after we had passed beyond this "boundary." With a hardly perceptible gradient, the wide plain rose toward distant hills. White clouds sailed in the blue sky—a long-missed and promising sight, for it was the first sign of rain we had seen for weeks. Herbage was visibly thriving here, thicker and much taller, and there were flowers. The farther we advanced into the North and the uplands, the richer became the vegetation; and many wild fowl and also some gazelles started up at our approach.

We pushed on through the virgin grasslands without stopping at a speed of twenty-five to forty miles an hour, in spite of mounds and hills rising in close succession, until we had travelled perhaps a hundred and twenty-five miles from our base—not, however, in a straight line, for I (who had the wheel) had made many a wide detour to avoid the enemy's tents. Now and then we had sighted enemy bands, sometimes appearing with startling suddenness, and had been fired at. But we were always out of range, and without being harmed or having to answer the fire, we reached, in the afternoon, the pastures of Nethel in the upland steppe among the northern hills of the Abu Rijmeyn.

We stepped from the car into a green sea of waving grass and flowers. The wind blew to our nostrils the sweet smell of this lush land. Deeply we inhaled the sweet air and with longing eyes gazed at the distant cause of all this fertility—heavy rain-clouds which had risen on the horizon. Faris spread out his arms as if to embrace it all.

The tall green blades of delicate grasses swept about our shepherd's cloaks. Above us a lark soared rapturously over a flowery hillside, while at our feet chirped the crickets. How good the mint and sage smelt! In silent gratitude we stood knee-deep in this paradise.

Faris walked away, slipping his *aba* from his shoulders. Then he stopped and contemplated this awe-inspiring steppe, the meadows over which brooded the arcadian peace of Arabia. There he stood alone and apart, like a Prince of Kedhar, whose tents and camel herds cover the hills of Midian and Ephra.

His gaze swept this abundance—the promised land—which in imagination he saw peopled by his *Bedu* and their herds. And then his head drooped. How can I express what passed through my mind as I looked on the bowed figure amidst the verdure? "Let Ishmael live before thee," I cried involuntarily. Faris was grieving for his people, amongst whom he was only a stranger, his head bowed down with the awful tragedy of the dying grasslands down yonder on the parched plain, where our famished tribe was wandering. A slight shudder ran through his body; he dropped to his knees, put his face into the grass and stroked caressingly the beloved earth. Yearningly he cried: "*Ya ummi*—my mother!"

The wilderness was his motherland, rich, beautiful, most dear, for he had never known cities.

Before we started homeward, Faris tore up bunches of grass by the roots; each one of us had to take back an armful to testify to the fertility of the land we had explored.

When we reached camp we found hundreds of men seated before the threshold of Tra'd ibn Sattam's tent, waiting for our tidings about the land in the North. Slaves brought up dry brushwood and herbage and piled it on the slumbering fire. Soon the flames were crackling, leaping as high as the roof, and the inside of the black tent was one red glow.

We spread out our silent witnesses—the bunches of grass, herbage and flowers, which were no less precious for being withered. All night long the people came, even from the most distant camping-places, to see and touch them. They fingered the long grasses with exclamations of joy and praise to God. Now and then Tra'd ibn Sattam handed out a blade, which passed from hand to hand, and some would lift it to their lips with a murmur of *"Ya hayat*—O Life!" And each time Ibn Sattam proffered one of these precious specimens from the grazing grounds of the enemy, he would say: "Here are the proofs of Life. Tell your children that we shall go on." And the tribesmen vaulted on to their horses and galloped into the night, to show the emblems of hope to their women and children and neighbours, and to tell them of the wonders of the highland pasture.

The evening of the following day I sat talking with some Ruala by the fire in the principal tent, with others coming and going, when a well-known voice called for coffee. Unnoticed by any of us, Amir Fuaz had entered and sat down. "Thank Heaven you are back," I exclaimed. "I'll gladly surrender my position to you"; and I offered him the place of honour.

Fuaz had returned from Rutbah empty-handed. The suspicion of treachery on the part of Yassin Bey had indeed proved groundless; but the French insisted on their previous decision and the English expressed lack of interest. Nothing had been gained.

At this juncture I proposed to Fuaz to let me try to bring about an understanding with his Bedouin enemies, but it was only with much difficulty that he could be moved to give his assent—not that he had anything against my personal interference in the affairs of his tribe, but because he feared that such a step towards conciliation would be interpreted by the enemy as a sign of weakness. It was only after I had talked to him for a long time, trying to ease his mind, that he said quite suddenly: "Well then, in the name of God, go to Ibn Meheyd. Was not my brother-in-law always thy friend?" He sent for Mijhem (his half-brother) and Faris, and instructed them to accompany me on my mission. For our bodyguards he detailed Mnahi and a friend of Faris, one Abd el-Karim, a Wuld'Ali chieftain from Syria, and the latter's slave, Sleyman.

We used Nuri Sha'lan's open car for our trip, and we avoided all camel-riders, especially when they had horses with them.

Early in the afternoon we sought out a secluded wind-sheltered position at the foot of a rugged hill, and gathered roots and dry weeds to make a fire by which to roast the bustards shot on the way by our slaves. The roughly plucked birds were cut into pieces, which were thrown on the hot ashes. The crops and intestines still full of partly digested herbs and red-haired caterpillars were also roasted in this way, and eaten with relish as a delicacy.

It was our intention to rest here awhile. From a point above our camp we surveyed the surrounding country from time to time for wandering herds, mounted Bedouins or automobiles, but as far as we could see there was nothing living within view; the wilderness stretched away to the horizon undisturbed.

As we chaffed and laughed over our meal, six savage figures stood suddenly before us, as if they had risen out of the ground. They could not have ridden upon us, for Mijhem and Sleyman had, but a moment previously, scanned the whole neighbourhood with field-glasses. The six fellows must, therefore, have crept up on hands and knees from some spot close by, where they had been lying in hiding. They had no rifles, but nevertheless, they had us covered with pistols which they held under their cloaks.

At first they did not speak, and not one of us dared to move. Two of the strangers then commenced to argue with each other, eyeing us the while in a most unfriendly manner.

Unmounted wayfarers met in the desert in this way are usually common robbers and murderers, who will stop at nothing to attain their purpose. They have nothing in common with those worthy camel and sheep raiders who ride *dhaluls* and mares, and whose exploits are somewhat in the nature of knightly enterprises.

Faris and I exchanged glances and stealthily groped under our cloaks on the ground for our rifles.

Now I could take my courage in my hands and speak to our uninvited visitors.

"What do you want of us?"

"God knows."

"And how did you get here?"

"From over there."

"And where are you going?"

"Over there."

"What tribe do you belong to?"

"The Beni Adam" (Children of Adam).

The replies sounded impudent and dangerous; but we were used to desert ways. By their ambiguous replies, the strangers stamped themselves as ordinary robbers. Had they responded to my questions more openly, they would have made themselves and their tribe responsible for our safety (or our death). We could then either have removed our headgear or in some way have touched one of them, and thereupon claimed their protection. Even to spit on a man (a truly singular way of "touching") and thus call on his protection is permissible and efficacious enough to save one's life, if not at the same time one's property.

These fellows had no use for the honoured customs of the Arabs. They were responsible to no one and would kill us in cold blood. Why they held back was incomprehensible.

As a last resort, and in order to get some idea of the strangers' intentions, Mijhem offered them cigarettes. They shook their heads in refusal, but their attention was momentarily distracted from us. Like lightning Faris seized the opportunity to raise his rifle and fire over their heads. Mijhem and I, who had awaited a cue, fired from under our herder's coats.

The surprised thieves fell back in fright. Two immediately threw themselves on the ground, while a third let off his pistol at us. The bullet lightly grazed Sleyman's left forearm, and he promptly pulled the trigger of his rifle and shot the robber in the thigh.

Mijhem and Faris ordered the bandits on whom we had so turned the tables to throw off their cloaks and face the other way. They obeyed without a word, and as the *abas* fell from their shoulders, we saw that each man's belt carried a small arsenal of daggers and pistols. They were ordered to place back in their holsters the pistols with which they had threatened us and to throw their belts to us.

These six worthies belonged by origin to the tribe of the Duleym. Faris got this out of them by a searching cross-examination; also, that, as the Duleym were confederates of the Fid'an, they were on the way to these allies to procure camels and horses. Lazy footpads like these carry no rifles; they find small firearms suit their purpose better.

They now revealed quite frankly that they had taken our automobile for that of the Sheykh of the Amarat. That a fighting-car of the Ruala might be in enemy territory had not entered their minds. Only our black or brown herder's coats betrayed us on closer view as possible foes.

We thanked our lucky stars for this error which had saved our lives and sent the robbers on their way unmolested, but without arms and ammunition. The wounded man we carried with us to the camp of Ibn Meheyd.

Before they left us, these fellows had the impudence to ask us to make a detour and take them into the neighbourhood of a Saba camp which they intended to raid. Incorrigible rogues!

"But the Saba are your allies!" I cried out, astonished.

"What of that?" answered the leader. "Thou are *gûm* (enemy) of the Saba."

"Magnanimous Duleym!" said Mijhem ironically, "thou art in error; we are on a peace mission."

"Allah! How fastidious art thou!" responded the man, with equal irony, and turned his back on us.

Our head-cloths fluttered in the wind as we raced on again over the undulating plain. Small groups of riders on camels and on horses appeared from time to time. They stood still as we passed, observing us from a distance.

We had also noticed three automobiles which held a course parallel to ours for some distance, but disappeared now and again behind a hill or in some depression. After one such disappearance, they reappeared much nearer to us. We halted and signalled to the motorists. They circled about us with rifles ready for action. Then they got out of their cars and advanced towards us, with their rifles cocked.

As they approached, they yelled out that we were spies who had come to reconnoitre their land and camps. One of them recognized the wounded Duleym and began to question him, but the man remained silent, except to say that he would speak only before the *sheykh*. I overheard a few words which clearly showed that we stood in danger of immediate death. I thought it wise at least to warn their Akid.

"We are in Syria. Not only Ibn Meheyd, but also the Fransawi (French) will hold thee answerable for our safety!"

"Then prove thy friendly intentions," he answered.

I proposed that we should accompany him and his men to their camp.

He accepted my proposal only after we had handed over our rifles; our pistols we were allowed to retain.

Following our enemies, we drove in a northeasterly direction. After a few miles we met the first herdsmen and their flocks and herds, and half an hour later the great camp of the allied Fid'an, Saba and Amarat Bedouins came in sight—tent ranged by tent in vast array. All the while new families with pack-camels came in and took their places on the wide plain, while women and slaves hastened to raise the black tents.

A young acquaintance of Berjas ibn Hedeyb rode up to us and recognized me. He accompanied us to the large council tent of the assembled *shiyukhs*, and on the way related that a few days earlier some Fid'an had visited the grave of the old Hero-Chief, Turki ibn Meheyd, at Aklat Suab.

As an offering to the memory of his forebear (Turki was killed in battle against the Ruala, although his daughter Turkiyye was married to the Ruala chieftain, Sattam ibn Sha'lan) Ibn Meheyd had sacrificed a fat camel over the grave: "So that Allah might read his heart and give him victory over the Ruala." This is a heathen, pre-Islamic custom of the Arabian Bedouins.

It would seem that Ibn Meheyd and his vassals had made not only material, but also spiritual preparations for a decisive war against the Ruala.

Our enemies were now assembled, and the conference of the chiefs was in full swing when we arrived.

Ibn Meheyd looked aged and the bitterness of his thoughts had hardened his features. This unpleasing impression was deepened by his beard and eyebrows, which he had dyed black.

A thick woollen shawl enveloped his head and throat, despite the warm sunny day. He had been a sufferer for years from a wasting fever which he, like so many other Fid'an Bedouins, had contracted in the unhealthy lowlands of the Euphrates.

On our appearance Ibn Meheyd had risen and taken a step forward, but on recognizing the familiar faces of his enemies, he turned back and beckoned to the leader of his Negro bodyguard. Even to me he had not given the customary salute, but only swept me with a black look. Fortunately, I perceived at once that we had put our heads into a hornet's nest, and I whispered to my friends on no account to step within the circle of the *shiyukhs* without me.

No word of greeting or otherwise had come from these. Some turned away with ostentatious disdain. Ibn Meheyd, with his back to us, was excitedly whispering into the ear of his black body-servant, who was listening with bent head. The men of the bodyguard stood with eyes fixed on those two, their hands round the butts of the pistols in their belts, ready to draw.

Meanwhile, more by instinct than design, I seated my-self close to Ibn Meheyd and motioned Faris and Mijhem to sit down too. (Abd el-Karim and the two slaves were waiting in our motor-car.) Furious ejaculations burst from every mouth at the liberties I was taking. At the sound, Ibn Meheyd turned in surprise; silently he re-garded Faris and Mijhem with lowered brows and sinis-ter eyes. I divined, nay, I could feel the murder in his mind. One sign from him, and there was an end of my friends; perhaps of me too.

There was not the fraction of a second to lose. Hailing the despised "coffee-cook" by the hearth, I called out to him: "O boy—strength to thee!" The old Negro looked up, startled, but did not dare to answer me; he only rolled his eyes timidly back and forth between me and his master. Suddenly Ibn Meheyd made a sign and his guardsmen drew their pistols. The last fragments of my courage and self-possession dropped from me and my knees trembled. But—the pistols were not levelled. Faris and Mijhem had been quicker than the guard. With great presence of mind they had whipped out their re-volvers and had Ibn Meheyd covered before the blackamoors could take aim. And this they dared not do now.

This coolness helped to restore my own composure and I cried to the cook reproachfully:

"Is it forbidden in the house of Ibn Meheyd to present the cup of peace to the guest who has alighted at his sanctuary?" The old Negro dithered, as he reluctantly reached for the small china cup that was placed upside down on the handle of a big coffeepot to dry; he turned his face anxiously towards his chieftain. Unwilling to wait any longer, I jumped up and went quickly to the hearth, helped myself to the cup, took the pot from the bed of glowing embers—it burned my fingers cruelly, but I bit down the pain—and poured out the customary measure. Then I went up to Ibn Meheyd and presented the cup to him with the salutation of peace. He looked at me with bowed head from under lowered lids.

He must obey the Law of the Desert; he must take the proffered cup. Nor could he play with the lives of my friends without forfeiting his own. At the first aggressive move, he would be riddled with bullets, for Faris and Mijhem still had their pistols trained on him. He turned from me, but I put my hand on his shoulder: "Peace!" I said. He turned round again, a fanatic light in his eyes; but, despite the angry face, he now opened his lips to bid me peace and asked me to sit in his own seat.

Then, and not till then, Faris and Mijhem dared to put up their weapons; the word "peace" had been formally pronounced by the host. Slaves heaped cushions for us against the camel-saddle.

Ibn Meheyd himself then took the coffee-cup from

the slave's hand and presented it to me with, "Welcome! May it please thee!" Twice he repeated these words, which are a guarantee of peace and safety. Then Faris and Mijhem also drank with him.

To us, used to the ways of Western civilization, such a train of events and their result must seem incomprehensible. But after one has lived a length of time with the Bedouins, one learns to understand that the unwritten laws of the Bedouin social code are closely adapted to the conditions of life in the desert and have sufficed, from time immemorial, to meet its manifold circumstances. Without these rules of the game, indeed, all human life in nomad Arabia would have become extinct long since.

After I had asked, and Ibn Meheyd had granted me, leave to speak, I set forth the object of my mission and exhorted the assembled *shiyukhs*, with what persuasive eloquence I could muster, to make peace with the Ruala, and, as in former years, share the grazing-grounds like brothers. I dwelt on the advantages of unity and the evils of dissension, and drove home my argument by pointing out that by their present policy they were only playing into the hands of foreign powers, who, after all the Bedouin tribes had been weakened individually, would encompass the complete destruction of them all.

My exhortations and arguments were received in cold silence. Most of the chiefs sat with bent heads and tapped the ground with their camel-sticks in apparent boredom. I felt pretty sure, however, that their indifference was assumed, and I would not let myself be discouraged. Once more I returned to my task and, mustering all powers of persuasion, I redoubled my effort to bring the benefits of good will and a just peace before their eyes. At length I succeeded in persuading them to abandon their hostile silence and to enter into a sort of discussion with me. But anyone who believes that Bedouins can be persuaded at short order is mistaken. Hours passed. It was close on midnight, when Faris begged to be allowed to speak in the name of Amir Fuaz. Ibn Meheyd nodded. "Peace!" said Faris. "Truly, the Enemy of Life is pressing back the living. The milk from the breast of the desert has turned into dust. Like bitter myrrh does it taste to them that thirst. Our wells are dried up, our pastures are scorched by the sun, our camels are perishing in the land of hunger and thirst, thousands are dying on the paths of the earth. Praise unto God that he still keeps his hand open above your heads, but to the Ruala he has closed his heaven. Far be it from us to come as enemies. We would enter your grassland as your guests."

The words made a deep impression. Faris had spoken as a Bedouin. He had spoken a language they had all understood.

The *shiyukhs* withdrew. For perhaps a half-hour they stood under the stars, among camels, horses and sheep, debating and gesticulating. Then they returned and in silence seated themselves in a circle by the camp-fire. Only Rakan, the Chieftain of the Saba, was missing—an indication that he must have fallen out with Ibn Meheyd and the others with regard to the peace conditions. We knew him to be the wiliest of our enemies and the idea came to me at once that he would try to ambush us on our return journey.

After the coffee-cup had circled once more, Ibn Meheyd leaned back on his cushions and said solemnly:

"O ye assembled ones! It is our wish to keep peace with the Ruala. But it is God's will that there is war between Fuaz ibn-Sha'lan, Tra'd ibn-Milhem (Chief of the Wuld'Ali) and our *shiyukhs*. We decree therefore that there be peace between the tribes, but war between the chieftains."

Thereupon Ibn Meheyd offered me his hand. I grasped it and thanked him and the others in the conclave for their willingness to share their grazing-grounds during the coming summer with the Ruala and Wuld'Ali and for allowing the peoples to live side by side in neighbourly amity. I also expressed my hope that the belligerent chieftains would also soon conclude peace among themselves.

It would have been useless to waste more words on the healing of the breach between the *shiyukhs*. If Ibn Meheyd fulfilled their promise of peace between the tribes, I could be more than content with the result of my journey. It would be no less than a miracle.

It was still dark when I was roused from sleep by the clatter of cooking utensils. The cook was just putting his water-pots on the glowing fire. Enveloped in its acrid smoke, by the threshold, stood the old mare that had carried me to this tent after the conference. I stepped into the open. It was still night, but the stars were paling and in the east the greenish-grey of dawn mantled the desert as with a fine veil. Between the tent-ropes lay our host's camels, chewing the cud. Beyond them spread the softly undulating steppe, and a wonderful fragrance exhaled from it. Everywhere was a stillness and a peace which filled me with awe.

But where were the tents and the herds that at midnight had covered the whole neighbourhood?

I ran into the open a little way and looked about. Far and wide no other tent. Our black shelter lay like a derelict ship on the ocean.

A curious feeling of loneliness came on me for the first time in my life among the Arabs. I had been left with a few companions only, where the evening before thousands had camped round us. Silently the Bedouins had broken camp and they—their women, their children, and their animals—had melted away like a mirage; I could not understand it all.

"Faris! Mijhem!" I called and went to wake the sleepers. Sheykh Nauaf-es-Saleh, in whose tent we had slept, also appeared. I took his hand and asked:

"What does this mean?"

"What doth it mean, thou askest?" he replied. "Ibn Meheyd never breaks his word. The promise he made thee last night he fulfils even this morning."

Ibn Meheyd had evacuated his grazing-grounds to make room for the Ruala!

Nauaf pointed to a group of persons some distance away, now visible in the stronger light. They seemed to be resting, just about where Ibn Meheyd's tent had stood the previous evening.

We rode over and found Ibn Meheyd himself, with

six men of his bodyguard. They rested on their rugs, Bedouin-fashion, on crossed legs. Beside them was a heap of dead ashes and the three soot-blackened stones on which last night the cook-pots had stood. A brass brazier shed a little warmth, comforting in the chill of the morning. Ibn Meheyd sat holding the wide sleeves of his cloak over it.

He stood up at our approach and, when I had dismounted, he came up to me and put his arm paternally round my shoulders. "My son," said he pleasantly, "dost thou see that Ibn Meheyd has been true to his promise?"

His eyes said more than the few words. I seized his right hand and pressed it gratefully in both my hands. "May God grant thee all thou wishest!" I said in farewell.

"Come to visit me this summer," he called after me, "and pitch thy tent with the Fid'an. Thou art indeed a Rueyli, but we count thee also as one of us. God be with thee wherever thou goest!"

☙ XIX ☙

The Ambush

O N OUR HOMEWARD drive to the Ruala camp, only an
hour or so after we had parted from Ibn Meheyd,
we were attacked by Bedouins from ambush in a *wadi*.
The ensuing action was brief, but it cost the life of
Abd el-Karim, who was particularly dear to Faris, while
our assailants left three dead behind. They proved to be
Saba of the House of Rakan.

Abd el-Karim's end was most harrowing. Sitting
directly behind me in our open car, he was fatally
wounded by a bullet which tore his abdomen to pieces.
Realizing the inevitableness of the end, he calmly ordered his slave to shoot him through the head, before our
very eyes. We scraped a shallow grave for him in the
sand, and we were still occupied with the other dead
when Sleyman, who had been posted on guard, reported
that he had sighted three motor-cars through his binoculars. They were trying to cross the *wadi*, a considerable
distance off, and come up on our side.

We pushed our car to a covered position in the *wadi*
and made ready for action. The Saba were coming towards us cautiously. The visibility was bad in the dazzling glare, but at last we scored some hits, and the
enemy fell back beyond reach of our long-range rifles.

While Faris and Sleyman kept watch on our opponents' movements, we others set to work to change the
tyres riddled in the earlier fight and to solder the dam-

aged radiator. This of course we could do only very patchily; but luckily we managed to drive the heavy car out of the riverbed and make for the enemy.

The Saba divided on our approach, obviously for the purpose of attacking us on two sides. Mijhem steered for the car on our right, which had wheeled suddenly and stopped broadside on. Its occupants raked us with a hail of bullets, but although a number of these hit our car, we managed to dash in closer. Our carbines answered shot for shot. Steel rang on iron, the wind blew out our cloaks, bullets whistled past, sand and pebbles spattered my face, and wild shouts came from my companions; but I thought there must be some wounded, for our fire lessened. (Faris, Mnahi, and Sleyman had in fact been wounded more or less seriously, but carried on as well as they could.)

With a fresh volley of steel-cased bullets, we finally put this carload of our opponents out of action. If they were not all dead, we could feel sure that none were left fit to fight. Indeed, we drove up to within a hundred yards without drawing a shot. But now it was high time for us to turn against the other two cars, which appeared on our left, already dangerously near.

We headed for them, but we had gone little more than a mile when our damaged engine stopped abruptly.

There was no time, of course, to attempt repairs. We could no longer manœuvre the car, let alone take to flight. "Get out," said Mijhem. There was nothing for it but to stand our ground, with the car for cover. It was then I found out how badly Faris and Mnahi were injured. Faris could not move his right leg, and I had to half lift him out of the car. It was a mercy that the two enemy cars did not attack at that critical moment. They must have suffered losses in the first attack more serious than ours, for they had retreated beyond our range, and were marking time, merely watching us.

I took advantage of this respite to get out my surgical kit and dress the wounded. My dear friend Faris was not so badly wounded as I had at first thought. The deep groove made by a bullet in the upper part of his right thigh bled profusely, but it was only a flesh wound. I cleaned it and closed it with half a dozen clamps. The bullet that had wounded Mnahi had gone clean through his shoulder and lodged in the muscles of his neck, and I easily succeeded in extracting it. Sleyman showed nothing worse than some harmless grazes on the wrist. I was bandaging these when Mijhem shouted to me to hurry. A fresh attack was coming.

I picked up my rifle and cartridge-belt and cowered down under the rear end of the car. I felt sick to the point of vomiting, and very weak; I could scarcely raise enough energy to throw open the chamber of my carbine and slide in a fresh cartridge clip. My nausea was perhaps due to the ether I had involuntarily inhaled when attending to our wounded. I felt better, however, after I had been lying for a while under the car with my carbine under my arm.

Meanwhile, the two hostile cars were drawing nearer. They drove one behind the other, so that only the leading car offered a good target. We pumped lead into its iron body, but unfortunately not with steel bullets; for Mijhem had brought along only a few clips of this ammunition and wanted to save it for the decisive moment —an ill-advised economy that was to cost us dear.

Presently the foremost car skidded, then reduced speed, and finally stopped six or seven hundred yards away. The car behind it, however, rushed on us at terrific speed, swerved sharply only about ten car-lengths from us, and was gone as quickly as it had come. The whole thing could have taken no more than thirty seconds.

In these few moments a terrible tragedy befell us, the details of which I fear I am quite unable to give with any degree of accuracy. I recall that at the critical moment I was chiefly conscious of the fact that only two or three shots were fired on our side. We had made the mistake of emptying our carbines almost simultaneously on the leading car. We all had to reload, and that allowed the other car those fatal few seconds in which to make its rush unchecked.

When the first car had stopped (really put out of action by our fire), I had not a cartridge left in my magazine.

As I started to load a fresh clip, I heard a dull thud behind me, and a heavy body tumbled over me. I jerked my shoulder to let it slide off, and it collapsed limply on the ground. It was Sleyman. His wide-open eyes stared into emptiness. A bullet had pierced his right temple and come out under his left jaw. At the same moment I became conscious again of the oncoming car not one hundred yards off, and heard a voice cry, half in terror, half in warning: "Merciful One! O God of Grace!"

It was Faris who had cried out. Only then did I notice

that he was no longer beside me. He had crept out from cover, to get a clearer sight, and was lying wholly exposed on the sand.

As the death-car thundered past, bullets clashed into the chassis of our vehicle, but in spite of the feverish excitement and the clanging and clatter about me, my ears picked out repeatedly in the fury of noise those dull, hollow thuds known only to those who have taken part in pitched battles—the sound of bullets striking into living flesh. Then I also heard moaning and groans. I straightened up a little to take a hasty look—and my blood ran cold. Faris lay writhing on the ground ahead of me.

My last shots spat venomously after the swiftly retreating car. Then I raised myself and, leaning on my carbine, staggered like a drunken man to my friend's side. He now lay quite still, with his face in the sand. I turned him over. His eyes were glassy, but he was still alive. Blood trickled from the corners of his mouth, staining his handsome face and his dress. Near him lay the slave of Abd el-Karim, riddled with bullets, a ghastly sight.

I fetched one of our water-bags in which we kept sulphur-charged water from Tudmur and with it washed Faris's face. He was quite unconscious; this made it easier for me to examine his injuries. Apart from the relatively unimportant thigh wound which he had received in the first attack, he had two terrible wounds in the right breast. To me it seemed a miracle that he was still alive. Both bullets had lodged deep down; to extract them with the means at hand was out of the question. I could do nothing but bandage the wounds with Mijhem's assistance.

Mnahi had broken down from sheer weakness and was huddled on the footboard.

Everything seemed unreal.

Together with Mijhem I started to collect the scattered rifles. We ejected the spent cartridges and reloaded and stacked the arms beside Mnahi.

As we carried our two dead to the car, Mijhem was also overcome by faintness. He dropped suddenly as if he had had a stroke, and remained full length on the ground. With my last remaining strength I got Sleyman's body into the back seat. Then I sat down on the running-board beside Mnahi.

I covered Faris with my cloak, for it was getting cool. I now felt thirsty and took the leather bag with the sulphur-water with which I had washed the faces of Faris and the dead men, and drank eagerly. That revived me. I picked up my Zeiss, for it seemed to me as if there were something stirring in the apparently disabled car of the enemy. I had not been deceived. The crew were obviously engaged in repairing their engine; I could clearly see three figures moving about. I handed the glass to Mnahi, asking him to keep watch on the enemy while I tried to restore Mijhem. He soon got up and tried to shake off his faintness. He drank some water and so did Mnahi.

There were two carbines for each of us. Four of these six we had loaded with steel-jacketed ammunition, and these we meant to use first. Mijhem had now recovered enough to stand by me. For Mnahi we made a seat so that, leaning against the car, he could take part in our defence.

The sun was nearing the horizon when the enemy car at last got under way. At first they moved away from us, but that was only to find smoother ground for their charge. We had agreed that Mijhem should open fire alone; Mnahi and I would hold our ammunition for the close fighting.

Mijhem shot steadily and accurately, but quite fast enough. I had handed him another carbine with steel bullets when, after his eighth shot, the advancing car stuck side-on, two hundred yards or so away. It must have run wild for the last thirty yards. In its front seat we saw distinctly the huddled figure of the slave. Of the rest of the crew there was no sign. All life seemed to have been extinguished.

Without a word, Mijhem, with rifle at the ready, started for the car at a run. I called to him to come back, but in vain; so I jumped up and ran to overtake him. After I had repeatedly shouted to him, he stopped at last to let me come up; and we advanced side by side, ready to fire at the slightest sign of life. The last fifty yards seemed to me endless, as step by step, every nerve taut, we approached the enemy car.

Nothing stirred.

The car was a ghastly sight. The three slaves huddled in it were terribly wounded and on the point of death; only the one at the wheel was still conscious. Mijhem drew his Mauser pistol, and, reaching behind the man, put a bullet through his brain. He then as quickly put the other two out of their misery, while I gathered up the men's rifles, revolvers, and ammunition. They all had been slaves of Rakan.

Meanwhile, it had become nearly dark. My eyes strayed to the tragic vehicle loaded with our dead and with Faris, as I thought, lying beside it, perhaps dying. Still and ghostlike it loomed in the gloaming. But, was I dreaming? Faris, whom we had left lying on the ground unconscious, was sitting in the front of our car!

He raised his hand and waved it at us! It was no hallucination! I left Mijhem standing there and ran to Faris.

When I sat down beside him, he slowly extended his right arm and laid it over my shoulder. So he leaned on me; and we rested awhile, side by side. I had switched on the lights on our instrument-board, and a faint glow fell on his pallid face. A sickly, sweet odour came from his blood-soaked garments. He tried to speak, but he was in much pain and could barely draw his bloodless lips away from his teeth.

When Mijhem had come back, we made ready to get under way. With some trouble we got our engine going. One of our head-lamps still worked and could be lighted; the other one had been shot to pieces.

I wanted to drive Faris straight to Damascus, where there was a number of French surgeons, one of whom I knew. But he only shook his head and begged us to carry him to his family and Tuëma. He was convinced he had only a short time to live and that no physician could help him.

I, too, had little hope of his recovery and ceased to persuade, feeling loath to assume the responsibility for his death far from his kin and without having seen his beloved one again.

"If we go now," said Faris, with pleading voice, "God will extend my time so that I may see Tuëma, and take her as my wife. And so I shall raise a 'name' to honour my father's house, even if it please God to take me away."

Faris—the true Ishmaelite!

Bedouins (and for that matter the Wahabees also) do not honour the tombs of their dead, but they revere the wombs of the living as blessed.

So we resolved to do the will of Faris. But, before setting our faces homeward, we drove to the Saba car and its three dead. We removed a good tyre and some parts, which Mijhem thriftily thought could be put to use, and also poured most of its petrol into our tank. What remained Mijhem splashed over the car and then set fire to it. As we drove away into the night, this funeral pyre lit up the dark desert and its unseen horrors.

We drove slowly and carefully,—it was morning when we came in sight of the Ruala camp.

⚙ XX ⚙

"The Cloud in My Eyes"

THE SUN HAD just risen when, from a ridge, we saw the black tents in the valleys between gently undulating hills. Some camel herds were already stringing out to pasture. I stopped the car and we looked at the peaceful scene spread out before us. The world could not be more beautiful than it was that morning.

On Faris's face lay the same still light that glorified the land. His eyes shone as with the gleam of a new light; and I was happy to bring him home.

To-day he looked on everything with the eyes of one about to say farewell. What at other times he hardly noticed, to-day he regarded with wonder, as if he saw it for the first time.

He asked me if I thought that the "other" life would be like this earthly one.

"Yes!" I replied. "But it is a life of peace and not of strife."

He looked at his bloodless hands. "Once upon a time they were strong," he said, "but now no strength is left in them. They are yellow like ripe seed. They will be laid in the earth." He looked into my face and said earnestly in a low voice: "Let us go to Tuëma."

As we made our way through the camp of the tribal division to which Faris belonged, a grave-faced throng pressed round our car and in silence accompanied it to his father's dwelling. Supported only by me and holding his head high, Faris dragged himself from the car to the tent. He would show no weakness. But the deathly pallor of his face betrayed his sad condition. There were also Mnahi's wound-dressings and the shot-riddled car to tell their tale. But though hundreds crowded close, grown-ups and children, and looked at us with anxious and in-quiring eyes, not a mouth was opened to put a question. The very dogs, usually so joyful and vociferous on the return of a party, were silent; they only snuffed the blood-stained car, laid back their ears, and slunk off as if they had received a beating.

Faris's father, informed of the disaster by the word that had flown from tent-row to tent-row, came in gravely and sat down beside his stricken son. It cost him a terrible effort to preserve the appearance of composure prescribed by the Bedouin code. He made no inquiry as to his son's condition until after coffee had been handed round, and even then he could only ask, according to established usage: "God willing, Faris, mayst thou stay with us?"

"I am alive, Father, God be praised! And there is peace."

"Peace?" asked Naif and some others in obvious sur-prise.

"Ibn Meheyd proclaimed peace in the council of his *shiyukhs*. Yesterday he had already removed his herds to the northern grazing-grounds."

"Peace—peace!" The cry of "Peace" ran through the tent and swelled outside into a chorus—"There is peace —we may move on!"

Behind Faris knelt his little sister and the small sons

of Tra'd ibn Sattam. Tears ran down the children's faces, but they bit their lips. Now our adventures were related, to the accompaniment of the free comments of the company. With incredible self-mastery, Faris, marked by death, sought to hide his sufferings and take part in the general conversation, which ran on and on. Every little detail of the fighting was threshed out in cold blood, and Faris's inevitable fate was discussed with (to anyone of the Western world) cruel disregard of his feelings.

This discussion lasted two hours. When the company finally rose, Faris also tried to get up; but a severe hæmorrhage threw him back on his couch, and he fainted. His mother was sent for. When he came to, she was kneeling at his side, with his hands in hers; and one could see she was hungering for a look from him. "My son!" she whispered, and kissed him, her face streaming with tears.

When Faris's still-wandering eyes saw her so convulsed with grief, his face quivered. "Who is this woman?" he said, propping himself on his elbow. "Take her away! I don't know her."

The slaves looked at one another uncertainly.

"Take her outside!" Faris called to them again. Then I took the poor woman by the arm and, with some words of consolation, led her from the tent. But at the entrance of the tent she wrenched herself from me, ran back and threw herself at Faris's feet. With both hands she gathered dust from the ground and poured it on her head and cried to God to preserve her son.

Faris touched her bent head and said:

"Go, Mother! God will give thee strength. I would have only happy faces about me. Nay, have I lived in order to be afraid of death?"

He motioned to me to lead his mother away.

When I came out of the woman's tent, a rider on a sorrel horse came galloping from another camp at the lower end of the valley and I waited. It was Tuëma, as I had thought.

Her whole body trembled and her voice was choked with tears. I tried to calm her and told her of what had passed between Faris and his mother. At this she pulled herself together and kissed my hands and pressed them to her wet eyes.

"What shall I do, Aziz?" she asked.

"Make his last hours cheerful, Tuëma. Show him that you are happy. That is all."

"Go thou before me," she begged, and tried to smile; but the tears rolled down her cheeks.

"Go before me," she repeated. "I want first to dispel the cloud from my eyes."

It had been decided that the marriage of Faris and Tuëma should take place that very evening. He had been inquiring after her with growing impatience. When I told him the glad news that Tuëma had come and would be with him at any moment, he begged first to see his mother again.

I went myself to the women's quarters to bring her. Her grief had made her a frail wraithlike creature: she walked with uncertain steps, but was more composed. She knelt down by Faris's couch. He put his arms round his beloved mother, and hugged her to his breast. Tears came into his eyes and they seemed to soothe the mother's pain.

She sat bolt upright by her son's side, arranged his clothes and cushions and replaited his long, thick tresses, which some words of jest about him and his beloved Tuëma. When she had finished, she left again, leaning on my arm, and from the threshold called out to her son that she would now send in Tuëma.

We had arranged a broad comfortable couch for Faris and partitioned it off with curtains; but one of them, according to the direction of the wind, was always drawn back, so that Faris, resting with the upper part of his body propped up, could look out.

A smile of happiness mingled with surprise suddenly lit up his face. Tuëma had come in. She had paused at the threshold with a smothered cry and a look of horror in her face at her lover's helpless plight. But so quickly had she mastered herself that I hardly noticed her emotion, and Faris saw only a smiling face as she moved to his bedside. Her silver bangles tinkled faintly. "Faris! Faris! My Life!" she exclaimed, dropping on her knees; and, twining her arms about his neck, she stroked and caressed his face and body.

When she kissed him, I noticed that her mouth was stained with his blood; but she kept her lips firmly pressed to his, so that he should not see that blood was trickling from his mouth on to her neck.

Shortly before sundown the tent began to fill with relatives and friends, who had been invited as witnesses to the wedding.

Tuëma had meanwhile returned to her own dwelling at the lower end of the valley. Her girl friends had been busy selecting the handsomest camel-litter and decorating it for the occasion. With its ornate marriage canopy it was mounted on a fine, gorgeously caparisoned camel, which slaves then led to Tuëma's tent. There the bride mounted to her lofty seat between the slender horns of the camel-litter and, with songs and shouts and waving of scarves, her girl friends escorted her to the tent of the bridegroom.

Before the women's quarters, but so arranged that Faris on his couch could see everything, Tuëma made her camel kneel down. Faris's mother and sisters, attended by numerous men and women slaves, greeted and received the bride ceremoniously.

Close by, Mnahi held an old white battle-mare by the halter. Auda, "the helper", she was called, and also the "Virginal Kuhaylat-Ajuz", for she had never been mated. The Ruala all but worshipped her as sacred. As a three-year-old she had been presented to Misha'il as a gift, on the birth of her son, Amir Fuaz. The mare was thus twenty-seven years old and her body bore the scars of many a raid. Over her back was spread a white lamb's-skin rug, the "Virgin Fleece" which, according to immemorial custom, the Bedouin bride brings to the bridegroom as a wedding gift.

Tuëma had disappeared into the harem to be attired in her wedding dress by Faris's mother and sisters. When she came out again, she was resplendent in a rich cashmere gown woven in red and green (it had been worn by Faris's mother at her own bridal ceremony) and a gold-laced shepherd's cloak floating from her shoulders. She took her position beside the white mare; and an aged Bedouin, with a little lamb, only a week old, in his arms, stepped before her, laid the lamb at her feet and slit its throat as a sacrificial offering. Auda snorted and backed away from the blood, but the old man grabbed the halter and, dipping his fingers in the lamb's blood, painted the *Wasm* (tribal mark) of the Ruala on the mare's neck. Then he calmly passed his gory fingers through his white beard. The slaughtered lamb was given, in accordance with the custom of the Bedouins, to an orphan—a little girl selected by a *sheykh*.

Without accepting a helping hand from Mnahi, which he offered because of her trailing garments, Tuëma lightly swung herself on to the back of the white mare and at a walking-pace rode through the camp. The huge Negro strode beside her, holding over her head the great sword of Janda and Jidua and exclaiming, herald-fashion:

> "See ye the bride of Faris! See ye the virgin!
> O for Tuëma's eyes and Alya's grazing herds!
> O for the dark hero and his bride!"

Thus the procession made the round of the camp, all the inhabitants of which were lined up in front of their black tents and, as the bride rode past on her white mare, it was with a joyful *"Zaraghrit"* they greeted her, even though their hearts were heavy within them.

Returning to Faris's tent, Tuëma dismounted, took the white lamb's-skin rug from her mare's back and spread it on the nuptial couch. Then she disappeared into the harem, to wait there until her bridegroom should call her.

Therewith the simple wedding ceremony was ended. We, who had been with Faris to witness the arrival of the bride, now rose to go.

The first stars were glittering over the hills when I stepped outside. The black tents in the valley melted into the deepening darkness of the evening.

The herds were wending their way homeward, their silhouettes now showing as they cross high ground, now sinking out of sight in the hollows. . . .

As my friends departed from the tent, each called out to Faris, according to Bedouin custom: "Vigour! And God be with thee!"

Behind the partition that closed off the women's apartment Tuëma was waiting for our going. When the last farewell was uttered, she pulled the middle tent-pole from its position and laid it on the ground. The roof bulged and drooped low in the middle, almost touching Faris's couch, but the lateral supports and the taut stays kept the rest of the tent fixed at about a man's height. It was the sign to any passer-by that a bride was with her bridegroom.

That night Faris died. When we came to his tent next morning, Tuëma was lying unconscious beside her dead lover.

A stone's-throw from the tent a few slaves were busy digging his grave.

As we committed our dear brother, lying on the white

fleece, into the keeping of the desert, the women looked on from a distance and bewailed the dead. Their hair was dishevelled and with smoke-black from their hearths they had painted signs of mourning on their faces.

Tuëma stood silent among them. The red cloak of camel-hair flowed from her shoulders. Her head was held high, but in her eyes were tears and a look of ineffable pain.

Once more the sun rose and beamed over the land.

The tent-poles dropped and the Ruala marched on. . . .

The living strode over the dead, marching on into the young morning to new pastures and to new life. . . .

Once more I rode on Sadha to the mound where we had buried Faris. It had already become a solitary thing —insignificant in the vast wilderness. A dog which lay on the grave slunk away at my approach. A bunch of white ostrich feathers was stuck between three fire-blackened stones which, the evening before, had formed Tuëma's hearth. This was her farewell to her lover. A gust of wind broke off one "flower" from this unfading wreath and blew it over the ground. I got off my mare to pick up this broken white feather and to keep it in memory of my dear friend.

I remounted and rode on, but presently pulled rein again and looked back. The lonely dog had returned to the grave: he turned round and round and finally lay down, curled up as if in sleep. He was mourning his dead master. Nobody minded him, nobody looked for him; but where should he be but here, with his dead friend?

I was on the point of guiding Sadha away when I noticed a rider coming in my direction—a Bedouin on a white-stockinged sorrel mare, who had just detached himself from a moving group of *kethabs* (riding-litters) and pack camels and was coming along at a tearing gallop.

It was Tuëma.

A short distance from where I was waiting for her she pulled up. Her horse snorted impatiently.

"Peace!" she called to me, lifting her hand.

"Peace, Tuëma," I called back. The tears came into my eyes.

"Shushan!" she called. The dog on the grave got up and walked slowly and reluctantly toward her, then stopped and turned his head.

"Shushan," she called again, and as she rode away, the dog followed her.

The Ruala were on the march and the land was covered with their camels.

Within a few days Tudmur was engulfed in the maelstrom. Day after day, with never a pause, fresh swarms of camels came out of the arid waste to stop at the foot of the hills and drink their fill. The sulphurous but wholesome water here issues from the hills in a clear stream, which branches out into a hundred rivulets in the plain and the small gardens surrounding the ancient city.

In the midst of the marching Ruala I rode again with

Amir Fuaz beside the *Abu Duhur,* the hallowed tribal emblem. But it all seemed so different now: no martial bodyguard; only the litters containing some chieftain's wives and children. Now there was no Faris among the young men galloping with them on their mares, with the baying greyhounds about him. In vain also did I look for the young war goddess.

The melodies of ancient herding-songs came floating back to us as we penetrated deeper into the beautiful pastures, which, with every step we took, became more luxuriant.

Never shall I forget that happy picture of the joyful people and its contented herds browsing, as they wandered onward, the juicy herbage and luxuriant plants.

Nor shall I easily forget the stragglers that vainly strove to reach Ishmael's promised Canaan. There were thousands of camels dragging themselves along with the futile exertion of the last remnants of their strength. They were still perishing by the wayside, while the more fortunate ones were already walking in the rich meadows that had saved them from death.

. . . .

Nearly two years passed, and the hardships of that spring were forgotten. Twice since then had I been with the Ruala, but only on my third visit did I fall in with the camp of the Shammar family of Faris ibn Naif; for in the rainy season the sub-tribes divide and wander sometimes hundreds of miles apart, and it is not so simple a matter to find someone you are looking for. On my arrival I was greeted by the sons of Tra'd ibn Sattam, whose tents adjoined the Shammar household, and after a while Faris's father came home, and we celebrated our reunion.

In a corner of the women's section of the tent there presently appeared a small, chubby Bedouin boy, who gazed at us newcomers with inquisitive and bashful eyes. He was still a toddler, and had to hold on to the end of the frayed tent-curtain.

"Menwer!" a woman's voice called from within.

The voice was Tuëma's; and this was Faris's son!

She came out and laughingly took the boy by the hand to lead him back, when I called out her name. She turned round in amazement and raised her hand to me in the salutation of peace. Then she bent down and whispered into her child's ear. The little fellow pointed to me and looked into his mother's face. She nodded encouragingly, and he wobbled toward me with outstretched arms. As I picked him up and hugged him to me, I laughed, but there were tears in my eyes.

Tuëma, who was speechless with amazement at seeing me again, at last joyfully exclaimed: "Aziz!"

At a gesture from her father-in-law she sat down on a camel-saddle beside us. She touched me with shy fingertips in greeting and in her dark eyes was the sadness of memory. Since Faris's death she belonged altogether to Ibn Naif's family. She had been taken into it as a daughter and sister.

She drew the boy to her breast, and the two fondled each other, a picture of maternal happiness.

"In the evening the Beloved one went from me," said Tuëma. "In the morning he came back to me."

"Sabah—the morning," I whispered to myself.

"Sabah" was the word Faris had said to her in farewell—
"Sabah—thou untouched morning, thou virgin bride."

Early the following day, I rode with Abu-Faris (the
"Father of Faris") to some rising ground. My eyes travelled over the Hamad, where the Ruala with their tents
and camels were migrating southward. I felt as if invisible hands were carrying off my friends into the
wilderness. . . .

"Is not the life of man like a tent and its dwellers?"
said the old Shammar Chief. "The day comes when they
go, and the site is forsaken. As Imrul-Kais says: 'Pause,
wanderer. Let us weep for the beloved one in his resting-
place in the shifting sand between el-Dujayl and el-
Hamal. He was like the evening star set in the midst of
the firmament!' "

This spring had brought back poignantly to my
memory that other spring, when Faris and Tuëma had
been together. It seemed to me now like a dream.

There arose in me (as it had in another great friend of
the Bedouins) the burning hope that always would there
be room enough on the earth for my Bedouins.

And as my eyes took in the earth and the sky, the
gentle hills and the far, far distances, the boundless expanse of the wilderness became peopled with recollec-
tions which, in spite of all that was sad, I count among
the most beautiful of my life.

◈ XXI ◈

The "Ark of Ishmael"

TO THE BEDOUINS of Arabia, the *Markab* has a significance such as the Palladium had to the Trojans.
They all hold the belief that the possession of this symbol, much like the Israelitish "Ark of the Covenant",
means safety and power to the tribe holding it, while its
loss spells disaster to the tribe and its subsequent disper-
sion. The Ruala have held it uninterruptedly for nearly
a century and a half, but even to-day the sight of
"Ishmael's camel-throne", with the chosen maiden sitting on it in times of war, will inspire them to greater
heroism. The warriors composing its guard of honour
are the picked troops of the tribe. They vouch for its
safety with life and limb; they are, above all others, the
heroes of Arabia.

Before coming into the keeping of the Ruala, the
Markab was held by the Amarat. More precisely, it was
in possession of the Ibn Hadhdhal family of that tribe
until 1793. In that year the Wuld'Ali, a tribe in alliance
with the Ruala, made war on the Amarat. Jidua ibn Mubadir, a Rueyli then visiting the Wuld'Ali, took part in
the campaign. At the height of the decisive battle, so the
tale is told, this Rueyli, with permission from the Wuld'-
Ali chieftain, flung himself on the horsemen guarding
the *Markab* (with the Amarat maiden enthroned in it),
cut his way through single-handed, and with one blow
of the sword cut off one of the legs of the camel bear-

ing the emblem of the tribe, and brought it to the ground. With the sudden overthrow of the Holy Standard, the resistance of the Amarat also broke down and, terror-stricken, they suffered a crushing defeat.

On the battlefield the victors found Jidua, killed from ambush by a foot-soldier, and the Amarat maiden of the camel throne—Jamila—who had stabbed herself to death so as not to survive the shame of her people's defeat. The Wuld'Ali, indeed, claim to this day that Jidua had been Jamila's lover; for, they say, the lifeless bodies of those two were found side by side beneath the collapsed *Markab,* and one of Jamila's hands was still clenched round the hilt of her dagger while her other hand clasped the hand of Jidua.

After the defeat of the Amarat, the *sheykh* of the Wuld'Ali presented the *Markab* and with it Jidua's sword, now famous, to the Ruala, since it was a Rueyli who had overthrown the *Markab* and thus brought about the victory to the Wuld'Ali. Since then this sacred emblem has been in the hands of the Sha'lan family and has accompanied the Ruala in all their victorious wars, a symbol of their dominant position among all the Bedouin tribes of Arabia.

Of Jidua's sword—Thu'l-Hayyatu—"the-one-endowed-with-life"—there is also an older legend, which the aged Prince Nuri Sha'lan thus related to me:

In the fifth century of the Hegira (the twelfth by our reckoning) when the 'Anaza Bedouins were still grazing their camels south of Teyma at the Jabal Bird, it happened on the sacred pilgrim's road to Mecca from Damascus. Janda ibn Mubadir, an ancestor of Jidua, was travelling with his clan toward Khaybar, seeking the *Dira* (pasture grounds) by the Jabal Abyadh and in the Wadi Rama. One still dark night, when the red camp-fires flickered in the tents, the air was suddenly filled with a terrific roaring. A mighty thunder-clap rent the sky, the ground trembled and swayed, and the whole world seemed to be tumbling. Every living thing leapt up in mortal terror and ran hither and thither. From the midst of the dark heavens above there broke forth a light that shone over the quaking earth with swiftly growing brilliance, until in a moment it had equalled the luminous power of the noonday sun and surpassed its heat. It blinded men and beasts and struck them down. The earth split; a sound of hissing, tearing, and crashing beyond the power of description filled the air, and a sulphurous smoke hung over the scarred earth.

When morning dawned it was found that many persons had been struck dead; their mutilated bodies were lying about. A crater-like scar marked the place where an unusually large meteorite had buried itself. In addition, a number of men and camels had disappeared without trace into the bowels of the earth, buried forever under sand and stones.

Janda ibn Mubadir and his war-mare, as well as two of his camels, lay dead before the wreck of his torn and partly burned tent. From opposite ends of the desert, from Haleb (Aleppo) in the north and el-Tayef (near Mecca) in the south, came reports that this exceptionally brilliant meteor, with its eerie sound, like "ker-ker-ker", had been observed, and that even the noise of its striking had been heard.

Some years afterwards some bolder spirits among the Bedouins nerved themselves to examine the hole torn in the earth. To their joy, these Bedouins discovered that the rift, widened and cleared by them, began to fill with water. Bir er-Ra'ad (the Thunder Fountain) they named the well. During the excavation, they found small fragments of the splintered "messenger-from-the-sky." A son of Ibn Mubadir took one such fragment from the meteor and fashioned from it a sword two and a half feet long. It gleams to-day as it did then, as if it were brand-new. It is of a bluish tint without one rust stain, and fine silvery wavy marks run down the precious blade, which is as light as a feather. A silversmith of Damascus made a handsome hilt and an equally handsome scabbard for it, and another artist engraved the blade with Arabic runes in gold.

"The Sword-of-Janda-and-Jidua" is thus, in the truest sense, a gift of heaven, and that is why it is called also the "Sword of God" and "The Life-endowed One."

When, at the end of that time of grievous famine, the Ruala had entered the life-giving pastures of the Fid'an and Saba, Amir Nuri Sha'lan presented me with this sword, to keep in remembrance of this adventure and my share in it.

I need not say how much I treasure it.

Part Two

HUNTING AND WARFARE

⚜ XXII ⚜

Ali, the "Protector"

AND NOW THOSE wonderful days with the Ruala had come to an end. I had to say good-bye for a time, because I meant to visit the Fid'an and other Bedouin tribes then roaming the deserts of Mesopotamia and Northern Syria. Several of their chiefs were inveterate enemies of Amir Fuaz, and at odd moments they also fought among themselves. But I knew some of them from earlier days and for the rest I pinned my faith on the inviolable rules of Bedouin hospitality. On the Euphrates I also hoped to find a suitable *rafiq* (courier) who would be qualified by his knowledge of the country and his friendliness with the tribes to act as both guide and guard to me. To assist me, Amir Fuaz gave me a personal letter to Hajem Pasha, who was then in command of the major part of the Fid'an in the Jesirah between the Tigris and Euphrates, while Ibn Meheyd contented himself with the lordship of the minority west of the Euphrates in Syria. Fuaz was closely related to Hajem Pasha, though these ties did not prevent the two chiefs from indulging in mutual pillage and warfare as opportunity offered.

Amir Fuaz advised me to go first to Aleppo and there get in touch with Hajem Pasha's *wukil* (representative), who would see to the transmission of his letter and secure a trustworthy travelling companion for me; and I acted on his advice. I had not been in Aleppo since 1916.

At that time I had vainly tried to find the sons of a *sheykh* called Achmed Hafiz, whose name will be known to readers of Homer Davenport's book, "My Quest of the Arab Horse" (New York, 1908). It was from this Achmed Hafiz that Davenport (with whose sister I became well acquainted in California) bought twenty-seven Arab horses in 1906.

On my arrival in Aleppo, my first task was to find the *wukil*. The directions led me to a mediæval building near the citadel. The entrance was barred by an enormous iron-studded timber gate. From the courtyard behind it I could hear the well-known guttural accents of Bedouins. I knocked repeatedly without response. Suddenly, however, with creaking hinges, the huge gate flew wide open, and out galloped four horsemen, almost running me down. Squeezed flat against a stone pillar, I looked in amazement after the small cavalcade that disappeared in a cloud of dust round the beetling ramparts of the old Crusader's castle.

When I turned my eyes to the entrance again, I saw standing before me in the doorway a Bedouin unusually big for his race, a good six feet high, who scrutinized me critically without "batting an eyelid" and without responding to my greeting. At length he coolly laid an arm round my shoulders and, in no very amiable manner, pulled me within, while with his other arm he gave a tug at a long rusty chain, which effectively closed the gate.

My eyes fell on a caravanserai that made me fancy myself back in the days of the Caliphs. The yard was not exactly tidy, but it looked better than many a khan

I had seen in Istambul and Baghdad. Scattered about higgeldy-piggeldy, in peaceful contentment, was a mingled assortment of camels, horses, asses, goats, and sheep. Lazily the lean, shaggy beasts munched the chaff spread for them on worn-out bast mats and hides. Cameldrovers, muffled in their frayed cloaks, were squatting about. Dirty children tumbled boisterously over the humps of the camels and darted in and out between their legs, while the animals, with blinking eyes and drooping ears, patiently put up with the sport. Pigeons continually fluttered between the court and the old bastions and turrets, and, sailing low over the battlemented walls, small vultures circled on motionless wings, croaking hungrily, with baleful eyes ever on the watch for a meal.

"Whence cometh thou?" the big fellow questioned without any form of introduction and with scant courtesy. I reached into my breast pocket and drew from it the letter of recommendation, much crumpled and stained, and with it, inadvertently, a photographic reproduction of Homer Davenport's well-known drawing, "Haleb's Farewell to the Desert." The picture shows Sheykh Achmed Hafiz and his Bedouin friends witnessing the departure of that celebrated Arab stallion, Haleb, which the Turkish governor of Syria had given Davenport as a present. My tall friend grabbed both letter and picture from my hand and fingered them clumsily. Suddenly he discovered on the photograph familiar faces and figures. A thunderbolt could not have produced greater consternation in the tranquil courtyard than did the giant's frantic exclamations at this sudden recognition. His surprise was comical. Stuttering with emotion, he tried to communicate not only to me, but to all and sundry, the startling fact that he had discovered his father in the picture. He behaved like a lunatic. He flung his arms about and danced round like a howling dervish. He laughed and cried in one breath and the echoes of his bellowing voice reverberated through the walls till everything seemed to shake; he *could not* calm down. His excitement communicated itself to the animals, and the whole company joined in the uproar. When peace was at last restored, I found myself in the arms of my new friend. Like the protecting wings of the Cherubim, the loose sleeves of his herder's cloak flapped round me, as he hugged me to his chest and kissed me on both cheeks.

"Thou art Davenport's son?" he cried, but it was more a statement than a question. I tried to explain, but in vain! He insisted that I must be Davenport's son, and would hear nothing to the contrary.

Gradually the man grew calmer and mutual understanding became possible. Ali was his name—Ali ibn Achmed Hafiz! And he was the eldest son of the *sheykh* in search of whose family I had come to Aleppo in 1916. What a stroke of luck, that fate should now present to me in the person of the *wukil* of Hajem Pasha the very man I had tried to track down from the time of the World War!

Reminded of my letter, he produced it from the capacious pocket, into which he had crammed it in his excitement, together with a lot of other papers, stuffed these back, assumed an air of importance, and said: "I am Ali, the *wukil* of Hajem Pasha, and Mijhem ibn

Meheyd, above all men." He cleared his throat and spat, as if all mankind were dirt. Then he continued: "And thou art in need of a *rafiq?*"

"That is so," I replied; "and this letter, which thou holdest in thy hands, thou wilt transmit immediately to thy *sheykh,* for it contains a personal message from Amir Fuaz."

Before I could prevent it, Ali tore open the letter and began to read aloud:

"Al-illah, by the Adored One! Peace be with thee, dispenser of protection! By the Dispensation of Allah, let this stranger live under thy countenance like a son of thy father. Befriend him as if he were my own eyes. Guard and preserve my brother when he lodges with thee or when thou settest him on his way. I would trust him to none but thee alone, who walkest with a clear conscience in the sight of Allah. May the Lord lengthen thy days, O thou rich in life, and let us evermore dwell side by side in friendship."

At this point, Ali interrupted his reading with copious supplications for heaven's blessings and rewards on Amir Fuaz. He had never suspected that the young Rueyli chief could be capable of such gentle virtues and tender emotions. He was visibly overwhelmed. He raised his voice and resumed:

"Praise thou the Lord! For He is so magnanimous and bountiful that He has bestowed upon me, His humble slave, so rich a gift. He, the Gracious and Merciful, granted me the wonderful opportunity of relieving thy ally and our brother, Barjas ibn Hedeyb, of seventy mares."

Ali jumped as if stung by a tarantula. In place of the previous outpouring of blessings there now issued from his lips a flood of wild imprecations and sulphurous curses on the head of the Amir. Again he raged like a madman. His outbreak was ably seconded by the other Bedouins, and once more bedlam broke loose in the court-yard, men and animals creating pandemonium. In their insensate fury, the men began to belabour the excited and frightened sheep, asses, and goats with their flexible camel-sticks, as if they had the hated Rueyli chief him-self under their hands. Even I, the innocent cause of this outburst of frenzy, became the target of Ali's choicest vituperation. How could I associate myself with such a notorious cutthroat and common bandit? It took a con-siderable space of time for Ali to calm down again—and with him the whole audience—and, in a voice still agi-tated, he read out the remainder of the letter:

"May the Lord take pity on thy saddened thoughts and may cheerful reflection on the Inevitable console thee and tranquilize thy soul." (I couldn't help laugh-ing out loud at this; whereupon Ali scowled at me most ungraciously. "All is fleeting, but all is also preordained by Allah. May the corpse of him who casts doubt on the bravery of my horsemen be flung aside without burial. God's infallible acts are manifest, and in the light of these events, which were inevitable, thou shouldst ac-knowledge the truth of my words." ("Aha!" I said to myself. "What a brilliant idea! To hold Allah responsi-ble for the theft of seventy mares!") "Allah bless my beautiful and virtuous kinswoman who is in the keeping of thy brother." (Tarfa, a sister of Amir Fuaz.) "May the position of the heavenly bodies be of better augury for thee! God is omnipotent!"

Ali, sunk in meditation, seemed disturbed by a thousand conflicting thoughts. At length, however, he dutifully kissed the face and back of this typical example of Bedouin diplomacy. Secretly, I had to admire the respect accorded in Arabia even to one's deadly enemy.

Ali grasped my hand. Anger still lingered in his eyes, but his voice sounded pleasant enough as he said to me: "This letter, my friend, is just about as good as a recommendation from Iblis" (the devil), and with a grimace of contempt he tossed it on the fire. I was only just in time to snatch the already singed sheet of paper from the flames; but, as a matter of fact, neither Ali nor I ever had the courage to present the letter to either of the Fid'an chiefs.

To my great delight, Ali offered himself as my *rafiq* for the journey to the Jesirah (Mesopotamia). Within two days he had ferreted out a second-hand Ford car to carry us to the Euphrates.

☙ XXIII ☙

Adventures with the
"Tin Lizzie"

ON THE DAY of our start, Ali tiptoed to my bedroom
at three o'clock in the morning, and whispered to
me to get up, as all was ready. No sooner had I followed
him outside than he forgot his consideration for the
sleeping caravanserai and bellowed like a foghorn across
the silent square: "O Ibrahim, get a move on!"

From the other side of the square came a sound of
spitting, hissing, puffing, and rattling. Our Ford had
awakened to life at Ali's shout and on wobbling wheels
was moving drunkenly over the rough pavement. We
could see nothing of it in the dark, but after a while a
dull yellow light became visible, which momentarily
flickered into greater brightness as it bumped over the
larger cobbles. Then, after a prolonged squeak, our
"desert-coach" drew up before us. The "chauffeur,"
barefooted but with muffled head and neck, alighted, in
spite of a pronounced limp, with a brave attempt at dig-
nity, but unfortunately he slammed the door behind him
too hard and it came off its hinges!

"Ibrahim," said Ali. With this one word he introduced
our driver to me. Ibrahim unwound three yards of thick
woollen shawl from his head and beamed on me with the
one eye he had left. A splendid match they made—that

old Ford car and he; small, lame, one-eyed, and the face heavily pockmarked!

I forced a smile, but inwardly I had a vision of the skeletons of Ali, Ibrahim, and myself bleaching under the wreckage of our car somewhere in the desert.

At half-past three we bumped our way into the wilderness.

On dry ground we covered about two hundred miles a day. We followed neither caravan route nor camel trails, but drove according to the directions of chance-met Arabs, some of whom would temporarily attach themselves to us as guides. Ali's knowledge of the country had given out after we had passed the market-place of Aleppo. But if I ventured to reproach him, he warded it off with an ingenuous smile and the declaration that he had taken me to his heart, and that he really could not let me travel alone.

He had indeed taken me to his heart, but at the same time he was quite ready for a joy-ride. It was his regard for me that was responsible for Ibrahim and the Ford. Goodness knows what profit he made on them!

We passed many nights in the open, but sometimes found shelter in some Bedouin camp. Near the Khabur River we found Hajem Pasha's camp. The old chieftain was very ill with severe pneumonia, contracted in the marshes of the Euphrates plain. I could only stay a few hours with him, and then we drove on towards Deyr-ez-Zor. From the first French military post I sent a doctor, who had Hajem Pasha transferred to Aleppo; but he died there a fortnight later.

In this wild region there was only one bridge by which one could cross to the northeast side of the river. After eight days we found ourselves in the farthest corner of Mesopotamia, not far from the Turkish frontier, and here we "cruised" about for days amongst minor Bedouin tribes. We passed dirty scattered villages with the sugar-loaf mud huts of Fellaheen, mostly Circassians and Kurds.

Their over-zealous headsmen and officials always tried to stop our progress. They seized our passports and kept us waiting while they telephoned or telegraphed to Aleppo, Raqqa, or some such distant centre, for information about us. Sometimes it was days before we could move on.

Taught by experience, we steered clear of the settlements, and this caused unusual excitement amongst the mounted constabulary. Once, near Hessedyi, we had a whole squadron after us. But even the best of their horses could not overtake our old Ford. They shot after us, but with no more effect than that the body of our car carried a few bullet holes as souvenirs.

When we had almost reached the main objective of our journey, the Tai' Bedouins, a stroke of bad luck befell us. A French machine-gun automobile held us up and took us to the newly built fort opposite the fortified Turkish town of Nisibin. The French commandant summarily stated that on account of an armed rising, the territory of the Tai' Bedouins was unsafe and his government could not be responsible for the security of foreigners in it, and that we must return to the Khabur Bridge—about one hundred and fifty miles as the crow flies. In addition, he ordered us to take as escort two Syrian soldiers into our already badly overcrowded car. The interview was short and sweet, and there was nothing for it but to submit.

In our tumble-down car there were now no less than seven men: Ibrahim, Ali, two Bedouin rafiqs, two soldiers, and myself; also a gazelle, a greyhound, and two hens.

We were packed like sardines: we had to hold on to anything that we could and change grips when the hand threatened to go to sleep. But with thirteen arms interlaced (Ibrahim's free arm controlled the steering-wheel) we prevented the car from falling apart, nor could any passenger fall out without the knowledge of the others.

All at once the car came to a stop. When Ali loosed his "frozen" grip, we all automatically detached ourselves from the collective embrace and tumbled out (literally), bag and baggage. After collecting the scattered bags, boxes, tin cans, guns, baskets, and pets, we turned our attention to the car.

Ali tore out the seats and everything beneath them that was not bolted and riveted. The two Bedouins unscrewed and tested the spark-plugs, and pulled out wires, for all the world like ribbons from a Chinese conjuror's blouse.

Only Ibrahim maintained a semblance of calm. He leaned with crossed legs against the front of the car and meditatively stroked a string of blue beads, which hung over the radiator cap.

"What is the object of those glass beads?" I asked.

"They bring good luck," he replied dreamily.

He then transferred his caresses to a bedraggled ostrich plume, stuck in the radiator cap.

"And this feather duster, what is that for?" I asked.

"This feather stands for strength, speed and endurance such as Allah has given to the male ostrich," Ibrahim replied impressively.

Now I knew!

Ibrahim twinkled at me with his one eye and with an air of superiority took the trouble in hand. Coolly he announced that the springs of the car had given away, and, still worse, that the front axle was broken.

"Then the 'wild ostrich' cannot run any more," I said sarcastically.

Ibrahim now lost his lamblike patience. He darted a look of scorn at me and angrily chased the volunteer experts away from his car with some highly original curses. The sleeping volcano had suddenly burst into activity. He replaced every screw, nut, spark-plug and wire which his "assistants" had pulled out. Then, with the boards of a box and strips of a gasoline can, he made a "splint" for the broken axle. For this job he needed also wire or rope, of which unfortunately we had only a few odd bits. Ali's shirt and my two (the only shirts amongst the seven travellers) had to serve as bandages for the broken limb of the "wild ostrich." As substitutes for the springs, Ibrahim cleverly fitted several padded boards over the rear axle. The result looked marvellous—but would it hold out?

We discarded all superfluous luggage, and even ate the two chickens.

After a short rest in the shade of the car, we proceeded cautiously and slowly, with many "Allahs", "Ahs", and "Ohs" over the fine, hard gravel.

By a miracle we actually reached the Kharbur about midnight. I embraced Ibrahim and took back everything I had said about his "wild ostrich."

☙ XXIV ☙

With the Tai' and Shammar Bedouins

LUCK FAVOURED US in eluding the vigilance of the French on our second attempt to reach the grazing grounds of the Tai' Bedouins under their *sheykh,* Muhamed Abd-er-Rachman at-Tai'.

His great camp spread out in a verdant valley, threaded by a long chain of rain pools. The snow-covered mountain ranges of Kurdistan, stretching beyond the Turkish frontier, formed a picturesque background. Camels and great flocks of sheep grazed over the desert, which recent rains had turned into rich pasture. Dotted about in groups were the black tents of the Bedouins. A horseman came to meet us. A foal, so it seemed in the distance, pranced round its mother, but as the rider drew nearer, we saw that the playful creature was a tame gazelle. The Bedouin rode a magnificent mare, that pranced on her feet like a dancer.

"Where is the abode of our host who will receive us?" I enquired. He pointed to the black outline of the largest tent, which showed from behind a ridge some distance away.

"Ha-wallah—by God—there dwells the Generous One!" He looked us over for a moment, then greeting us curtly, turned his horse and galloped away, the gazelle after him.

As we neared the large tent, the merry "ringing" of the coffee mortar bade us welcome. Malla Sulumeh, scribe to Sheykh Tai', conducted us within.

A considerable number of tribesmen were gathered in the roomy tent. As usual, the favourite falcon of the *sheykh* stood perched on a camel-saddle.

A slave removed the bird and placed cushions on the saddle for us. The coffee-cook poked apart the pieces of glowing desert roots on the hearth and poured between them dried camel dung from a fold of his cloak. He blew energetically on the hard nuggets, the size of walnuts, until small bright flames commenced to dance all over them. Then a large, beaked can was placed on the glow and it was not long before the coffee-water boiled and bubbled over. "Revive thy spirit!" said the every-ready cup-bearer as he offered me the aromatic cup.

Previously he had, in accordance with Bedouin practice, conscientiously wiped out every cup with the sleeve of his old shirt. Adroitly he held in his other hand four small china cups without handles, like so many eggs in a nest, and jingled them lightly one against the other.

The coffee made the round. The favoured guests, whom the Negro served first (unhappily I belonged to them) were the victims of especial politeness; before pouring the coffee, he spat first into the cup and wiped it dry with his shirt sleeve. Three times had I to endure this rite at the hands of the punctilious coffee-priest, who waited on us with the utmost solemnity on each occasion. Only then might I waggle the cup between my finger-tips in token of thanks and satisfaction and hand it back to him.

A tribesman entered the tent with the information that the chief's hunting-party was returning.

It was a wonderful sight as the horsemen drew up. There were about seventy of them, with hares, gazelles, and bustards hung over the withers and cruppers of their mares. A pack of greyhounds had been unleashed and they immediately sought the shade of the tent, where they stretched themselves out with heaving flanks and hanging tongues. Several slaves got up and brought them water, which they lapped up thirstily. Meanwhile, the riders had dismounted, and unloosing the casting-leads of the hooded falcons, set each bird on a padded perch before the rug of the *sheykh*.

Tai', on alighting from his horse, passed into the women's apartment. After a while he appeared before us. In honour of his guest, he had girded on an old sabre.

We all stood up and greeted him. Ali came forward and kissed the *sheykh's* hand, and pressing it to his forehead, said in his extravagant manner:

"Ya Muhafut—O Protector! God grant thee long life, most magnanimous of all Arabs!"

Then Ali presented me to the *sheykh*, who embraced me. With simple and grave courtesy he said:

"Peace be with thee."

With a polite movement of his hand, he indicated to me my seat and I sat down.

After we had settled in our places, Sheykh Tai' rolled a cigarette and lighted it between his own lips before he handed it to me.

Our host was a man nearly as tall as Ali, but very slender and small-boned. Rarely have I seen such refined hands and feet in a man,—in fact, his whole appearance was arresting.

For a Bedouin, he had an unusually pale complexion, set off by a brilliantly black beard and raven locks. He preferred to dress almost entirely in black. His Arab head-cloth, sandals, and soft camel-hair cloak were black, as well as the wide shawl wound round his waist. Even his mare was black, a rare thing, for most Bedouins hold black horses in disfavour. Headstalls, halter, saddle, and saddle-cloth—all were black, relieved only by delicate silver embroidery and a few silver ornaments. His silver-hilted sword, too, was carried in a black scabbard.

Sheykh Tai' was vain. He loved arms and horses, but above all he adored his little son, Farhan. According to Ali, he had not much affection for his wives, who were reputed to be beauties; but he was proud of them as he was of all his possessions—his great herds and extensive lands.

The Tai's Bedouins kept relatively few camels, but large numbers of sheep and goat, which suffer much from the depredations of wolves in winter and spring. Sheykh Tai' told me that these nimble-footed robbers from the inaccessible retreats of the Turkish Mountains had come down again into the snow-free lowlands. They had already attacked exposed Bedouin camps and caused great damage, although the watchful herdsmen had been continually on guard.

Sheykh Tai' was, like Nimrod, a "great hunter before the Lord", and liked nothing better than to be riding abroad. On the eighth evening after our arrival, he called a meeting of his sub-chiefs, and made known to them that he desired a great wolf drive organized for two days hence. Every tribesman with a horse was to join in the hunt, so as to provide a chain of beaters. Sheykh Tai' himself, his lieutenants, and I, armed only with lances, were to ride down the wolves and spear them. This was not the usual method of hunting wolves, but is certainly more romantic and exciting than shooting them with long-range rifles from automobiles.

When Sheykh Tai' asked me if I knew how to handle a *rumh* (the Bedouin lance) I had to own my ignorance; but it was not long before I learnt how to handle it under the tuition of my good friend.

These spears are from fifteen to eighteen feet long. They are of light bamboo, which the Bedouins cut in the swamps of the lower Euphrates. Below the triangular steel head they are decorated with tufts of the black and grey down-feathers of the ostrich, a few fluttering red ribbons, and tinkling coils of very thin silver chains. The butt is sheathed in a painted iron ferrule.

When at the appointed hour beaters and followers had lined up at the *sheykh's* tent, and all was ready, Sheykh Tai' rammed the butt of his lance into the ground and, using it as a vaulting-pole, leaped on his horse's back.

Besides Sheykh Tai' and myself, only the sub-chiefs carried lances. The rest of the men took their rifles with them, but merely to start the game and for defense in case of unexpected meeting with enemies.

Sheykh Tai's nine-year old son, Farhan, with a heavy Mauser pistol in his belt, accompanied us. His short, bare legs clung to the sides of an unsaddled mare, which he cleverly guided with his thighs and hands, and by his voice making her walk or gallop.

An hour before sunrise we rode into the steppe, waking to a glorious morning. I was mounted on a spirited mare, very fast and of great endurance. Over three hundred armed beaters from the widely scattered tents of the Tai' Bedouins had ridden out the previous day to the foothills of the Jabal Sinjar, there to cut off the retreat of the wolves into the northern mountains. Bands of gazelles and many bustards and other fowl fled before us. But we left them untouched, as we were after other game.

Only when the left wing of our riders roused two wolves did we give chase.

Wolves do not break cover and "go away" as foxes do, but there were other things to which one had to give attention in this hunt. Moles and burrowing mice had undermined the ground and more than half of our horses "took a toss" as they stepped into the hidden holes.

We galloped about twelve miles, and four or five wolves had been put up by the beaters. Our horsemen followed them tirelessly. I came so close to one animal that I could almost have touched his fur with my outstretched lance. My horse followed the runaway with the ardour of a bloodhound. I had therefore to give my undivided attention to the dangerous ground and repeatedly turned the mare aside, sometimes in the very nick of time, to prevent her floundering into one of the sandy burrows.

The slender lance rested perfectly balanced in my hand. My wolf slackened speed somewhat and my mare gained on him. In a few moments we were on top of the shaggy brute. He loped along with his head on one side, watching me out of the corner of his eye. He was cunning enough to keep always the same distance from my mare's forefeet and just clear of the point of my lance. If I urged the mare to a spurt, the wary old robber increased his pace just sufficiently—imperceptibly, but enough—to keep out of reach. At last, however, I thought my opportunity had come. With a vigorous thrust and a twist of the wrist, I aimed my spear at the wolf's shoulder. I put the whole weight of my body into it, so certain was I that I should spear him.

The tip of my lance actually grazed his pelt, but again the cunning old devil had the best of me, and slipped away from danger, and loped off. The lance drove full force into the ground and jerked me, as on a vaulting pole, high into the air. The shaft split into four parts, and I landed head over heels on the hard gravel beside my mare, which had come down on to her knees. Fortunately, the damage to both of us was trifling; a little skin grazed off, but that was all. I therefore mounted my good mare again.

Sheykh Tai', who had already speared one wolf, now joined the scattered group of riders to which I belonged. He threw aside his lance and, taking an automatic rifle from one of the beaters, galloped in pursuit of my wolf to prevent it getting clean away. With a long shot, he smashed one of its hind legs. The wolf tumbled over several times and rolled on the ground, snapping at the broken leg, until a second bullet ended its life.

Sheykh Tai' threw several handfuls of sand over the spilled blood—for so desert custom demands. Blood is *haram,* that is, "forbidden." Opening the jaws of the dead animal and pointing to the wicked fangs, he said: "Thou and I are kinsmen for the traces which thou leavest behind are the same as mine." (We are both robbers, he meant—like all despised Bedouins.)

Later in the day, as we galloped on, we sighted in the distance what at first we took for some of our mounted hunters driving wolves towards us. But they did not move.

I thought I could recognize riderless horses, watching us with raised heads. But Sheyk Tai' laughed and cried out to me that they were neither horses nor horsemen, but wild asses. I would not believe him at first, for the animals seemed too high in the leg.

Sheykh Tai' pointed out to me that the troop had a leader and this became apparent when the shy creatures ran off. We did not follow, and they disappeared into the clear distance of the Sinjar Mountains.

Fleeting shadows cast from above now hurried across the plain before our horses. I knew them of old from raids in the inner part of Arabia. They were the "Sharers of the Prey."

Shading my eyes with my hand, I looked up to the sky, where on motionless pinions the great vultures were sailing. They knew well the purpose of our ride; and they were sure of their feast of dead wolves. A wide-spread cloud of dust rose on the horizon and moved towards us. These were the beaters, whose semicircle steadily narrowed as it drew near. They started hundreds of gazelles that fled past us, but Sheykh Tai' and his men shot only a few of the fat bucks in their midst.

During the day's hunting, our party gave chase to fifteen wolves, of which nine were killed. One of them had made a kill of two gazelle kids, whose remains were still lying about. The mother, who perhaps at first had fled, returned and stood near by, bleating, as gazelles will. I could not bear the pitiful cries of the poor animal and gave her the *coup de grâce* with a bullet. It was the only gazelle I have ever shot, for I could never bring myself to kill these beautiful, graceful creatures.

It was evening before our body of huntsmen, laden with booty, arrived back in camp.

Three days after the wolf-hunt a slave of Mishal ibn Faris, Chief of the Shammar Bedouins, arrived, with an invitation to me from his master to visit him and his tribe, which was then camping south of the Jabal Sinjar. He also sent me as a present a golden-brown *aba*, such as is worn by the Shammar in Hayil. It was to serve as a symbol which would ensure a safe journey for me, and his slave would be my guide.

The Shammar and the Tai' Bedouins are hereditary enemies and their pasture lands are always, and were especially now, very dangerous regions in which to wander. Therefore, this was an act of particular courtesy and attention on the part of the old *sheykh* to give me safe conduct to his camp.

The following day I bade farewell to the Tai' Bedouins. Unfortunately, I could not accept the mare which their chieftain had offered me as a souvenir, for we had to travel by automobile. But I accepted two rarer gifts, and these heirlooms to boot. They were an ancient wood-carved coffee mortar, which had been in the possession of Sheykh Tai's family for generations. This pledge of his affection and friendship (as he called it) he had wrapped in an equally precious gift—three pieces of black cloth, artistically embroidered in gilt-silver thread, with verses from the Koran in Arabic calligraphy. They were choice pieces of the Ka'aba, which Sheykh Tai's great-grandfathers had brought many years ago from Mecca.

Loath as I was to accept such precious gifts, I was constrained to do so.

"We are brothers," said Sheykh Tai'. "Like the wolves. God be with thee. May He direct thy footsteps some future day into my dominions, so that I may meet thee again."

After bidding farewell to this wild, romantic and noble man, we cruised about in our old motor-car for five days along the southern foothills of the Jabal Sinjar, visiting the camps of various lesser tribes. Motor fuel we obtained from their *shiyukhs*.

Nowadays, nearly all of them own motor-cars, and on their migrations they carry a fairly large stock of gasoline with them on their camels.

At last we reached the wide plain through which runs the old historic caravan route from Deyr ez-Zor to Mosul and Baghdad. There we found the first outposts of the Shammar, and there also we parted from the faithful Ibrahim. I paid him handsomely and sent the man back to Aleppo, with his "wild ostrich", happy and contented.

Here, too, rain had fallen and transfigured the arid, yellow wastes into lush green meadows. From the small band of Shammar, our guide borrowed riding-camels for our further journey, and we reached the camp of Mishal ibn Faris on the following day. Of Mishal the Arabs say that "no cloud can be compared with him for generosity." I, too, must say that I have seldom met so unselfish and kind-hearted a man.

Outside his large tent we drew up and dismounted. How many guest fires must have been lighted under this smoke-blackened roof, which had sheltered three generations!

The elderly *sheykh* stood on the threshold and bade me welcome with the sacred formula of the wilderness, the assurance of peace, "Salam Alayk."

I responded in the manner of the desert: "God keep thee well." Then, Mishal ibn Faris took with his own hand the headstall from my mare and hung it on the main post of his tent. He had wanted to know me, he said, as soon as he had heard that a stranger, who loved Arab horses, was visiting the Tai'.

I thanked him for his pleasant and friendly invitation. In his way of addressing me there was more than ordinary politeness. From now on, whether with them in person, or far away, I had the freedom of his tribe.

Mishal ibn Faris, the great Shammar *sheykh*, esteemed from one end of the desert to the other for his staunch righteousness, had a peaceful and moderating influence on Bedouin politics, both in Mesopotamia and Syria. "A

man without a single enemy", Arabs have called him
to me.

I was Mishal's guest for several weeks. In the company
of his son Naif, I was able to look over a large number
of Arab horses amongst the different Shammar clans.
One two-year-old Saqlawi-Shaifi stallion of purest blood
pleased me exceedingly. One day I enquired of the
sheykh's secretary if he thought it possible that Mishal
would sell this stallion. It had indeed come to my ears
that Mishal had refused an offer of eight hundred gold
pounds from the French Remount Service. From my
experience, I knew that really thoroughbred Arab
horses were quite rare and therefore exceedingly expen-
sive. Considering the stallion's breeding, the French offer
certainly did not appear too high, when one remembers
that foreign military commissions and breeders have
paid in the desert anything up to three thousand pounds
gold for blue-blooded stallions.

I asked the scribe to submit my offer to his *sheykh* up
to one thousand pounds gold. I also declared myself
ready to make the customary presents to the *katib*
(secretary) and to the slave who had looked after the
stallion from birth.

That same day I sat with Mishal and his son Naif and
their friends until late into the night. By the light of
the campfire I showed them photographs of Arab horses,
among them the stallions and mares which I had bought
from the stud of Lady Anne Blunt's daughter in England, for the ranch in California.

"Is it known to thee," asked Mishal, "that Lord Blunt
and my father Faris formed a blood brotherhood fifty

years ago? He, as thou, loved our fast and enduring run-
ners, those 'Drinkers of the Wind', which Allah bestowed on our forefather Ishmael."

Neither the scribe nor anyone else said a word about
the stallion, and I dared not ask again; for I imagined
that Mishal was particularly fond of this young horse.

The day of my departure came. The patriarchal
sheykh and I exchanged words of formal farewell. Then
he led me aside and bade me sit down with him at the
farthest tent-peg. After a few minutes of silence, he
took two documents from a leather pouch and said: "I
have long noticed that thou hast taken the Saqlawi colt
to thy heart. He is the best of our breeding, and I am
happy to make thee a present of him, that thou mayest
always remember our friendship and noble horses. Take
the young stallion with thee and mention no thanks nor
price, so that this remembrance may live forever unclouded in our hearts."

"The Lord be good to thee, O Mishal ibn Faris," I replied, "for that I am allowed to part from thee with
such happy memories."

What more could I say in response to his simple
words? I knew the Bedouins. To be open-handed makes
most of them happy; and further, Mishal was a very
rich man. To him "belonged" not only the Shammar in
the Northern Jesirah (Mesopotamia), but he actually
owned sixty-nine villages and their cultivated lands on
the Khabur River. I could only hope that God would
grant me the opportunity some time of showing my
heartfelt thanks to Mishal in some special way.

One of the documents the *sheykh* handed to me was a deed of gift and a token of his friendship; the other set forth the pedigree of the colt. Mishal rose to his feet. He took me by the hand to set me on my way, and together we walked far out into the desert. He spoke no word and I made no attempt to break the silence. My eyes were held by the picture of the powerful young stallion which was being led ahead of us by Naif and a slave. Full of fire and grace, with prancing steps, he looked the living epitome of this wild and romantic land.

When some tribesmen rode by on their mares, the young stallion stopped still, his whole body tense, neck arched, and small head held high. His chest quivered as he neighed in long-drawn silvery notes. His uplifted tail flowed out from his croup like a cascade of water. He was surely as magnificent as any of those aboriginal wild horses, which, according to Bedouin lore, Ishmael caught in the Nufud desert. "Black-skinned antelopes (*kuhay-lan*) they were called of old, by reason of the black rims around the eyes, which make them look as if they had been painted with *kuhl* (pure antimony)."

The *sheykh* at last called to my companions, who had gone ahead, to halt. Looking back, Mishal and I saw the great camp a long way off. The old chief laid his hands in blessing on the forehead of the young stallion, and said to me: " 'Amud,' I have named thy stallion. It is a name of my people. The peace of God be with thee forever."

Then he kissed both my cheeks and the hoof of the horse, and strode back to his tents.

The French commandant at Deyr-ez-Zor had the two documents translated for me under his official seal.

One document, bearing the seal of Mishal, mentions Sir Wilfrid S. Blunt as the friend of Faris Pasha al-Jarba, and myself as Mishal's own particular friend, and certified that he had presented to me the Saqlawi-Shaifi stallion for love of me. The second document, setting forth the pedigree of the stallion, began and ended with excerpts from the Koran, the Hadith, and the Arabian poet Imrul-Quais.

It bore the seals of three Shammar *shiyukhs*—Mishal ibn Faris, Hassan al-Amud, and Jajan ibn Massiul, who testified regarding the horse as follows: "It is a Saqlawi, and we bear witness before Allah that the young stallion is a Shaifi, bred of a Saqlawi-Shaifi of the same pedigree; that the Grand-sire was a Saqlawi as was his dam a Saqlawiyah-Shaifiyah, whose noble race has remained pure and famous amongst us Arab people."

⚜ XXV ⚜

Honour among Thieves

AT DEYR-EZ-ZOR I was eventually able to arrange for the transfer of the young stallion to Egypt by way of Aleppo and Beyruth. It was a tremendous journey, as it had to be done on its own feet; but by slow stages the Arab, who accompanied the horse, succeeded in delivering him in good condition to my friends in Egypt.

Meanwhile Ali and I roamed further afield and rode to the pasture-grounds of the Fid'an, then camped at the northern foot of the Bishri Mountains, west of the Euphrates. There, also, the tent of Mijhem ibn Meheyd was pitched, and he received us hospitably. We spent several pleasant days with him.

He then led his tribe southwards into the Wudian area, east of the Hamad. We accompanied them through the Jabal Bishri and camped with them south of these hills. There I decided to say farewell to Ibn Meheyd, and bade Ali buy three especially strong *dhaluls* (racing-camels) and two mares. With Ali alone, and these animals, I struck through the Hamad desert, to make my way to the Ruala and to Damascus. On the first day we fell in with a small caravan of four men with twenty-odd camels and six stallions.

From this combination alone (for Bedouins never ride stallions on a raid) it was clear they were peaceful travellers. In fact, they were *Akhayl* or camel-traders from Inner Arabia, who had purchased camels and young stallions from various Bedouin tribes in the Euphrates.

Their kind is found everywhere in Arabia, Egypt, Syria, and Iraq. Almost invariably the *Akhayl* hail from Anayza and Buraida, two large oasis-towns of Kasim in the heart of Arabia.

During spring they travel among the nomad Arabs and barter rice, coffee, sugar, arms, munitions, and gold for camels and colts. Bedouins have only begun to sell mares since the arrival of the automobile, which has displaced the horse for raiding purposes.

These traders travel unmolested throughout Arabia and they pay the *sheykh* of the tribe from which they purchase animals a small sum for the privilege of pursuing their business. Each trader has his own special tribe which he visits every year.

On the second day, when we came on some rain water left in the rocky hollows of a *wadi*, we decided to rest awhile and let our mares drink their fill. We had hardly dismounted when two strange Bedouins on horseback suddenly appeared. Ali jumped on his mare's back at once, and deserting me and our animals, galloped away in the opposite direction from which the Bedouins had come, obviously seeking cover.

"A *ghazu!*" he yelled, as he rode away.

The two strange Bedouins were armed. They were obviously not traders, as Ali had immediately perceived. More horsemen appeared and they began to fire at Ali and myself. My "Powerful" protector, ducking low over his horse's neck, made a comical picture. The hostile Bedouins were Fid'an, as I knew from their striped shepherd's cloaks. To defend ourselves was useless, as we were surrounded. I threw my rifle on the ground and, dropping my arms with the palms turned outwards, I gave the Ghazu horsemen to understand that we meant to offer no resistance. When they came within hearing I shouted to them:

"We are *dakhil* (inviolable). We ride under the countenance of thy *sheykh* and our brother Mijhem ibn Meheyd."

But neither the leader nor his men took notice, but seized Ali (whom they had easily caught) and myself, and struck us for not taking off our clothing quickly enough. As Ali was being stripped, he cried to their leader:

"Hast thou no pity, plundering the friends of thy *sheykh* like this?" The man only laughed and said mockingly:

"I know not of whom thou speakest. We know nobody, and pity we have left to God alone."

"Thou wilt be answerable for this act," Ali shouted. "Hasten thou to return our property, our horses and camels, and take thy hands from off my friend, the guest of thy master."

In answer, the leader flung away the garment, the pockets of which he was rifling, seized his rifle and with its butt hit Ali such a blow on the back of his head that he fell as dead, and remained inert on the ground. The Fid'an's savage temper was aroused, and he continued to belabour the prostrate body with blows and kicks.

I sprang at the brute and tried to pull him away. One of his comrades, however, thrust his rifle into my back. I staggered, and before I could regain my balance, a hefty blow nearly broke my arm. The same blow caught me a glancing stroke on the head, hard enough to knock me out. I must have remained unconscious for hours. When I came to, the evening was already fading into twilight, and I found myself lying stark naked on the sand. Happily, it had not been a hot day, for the sky was clouded. Nevertheless, I felt wretched enough, and my head and arm ached. The blow had merely grazed the muscles of my arm, but I had a nasty wound over my temple.

Not far from me Ali was lying on his back. To my horror, he looked quite dead.

Still numb, I tottered over to him. Thank heaven, he was very much alive and able to talk. The Fid'an had handled him worse than me, but his unfailing good humour was already returning. "They have taken everything from me," he said, "except their cursed lice"; and he commenced to scratch himself all over his naked body, protesting the while that he had left Aleppo quite clean.

"The sunburns are itching," I said, with a laugh; "it cannot be the vermin of our friends."

In the deepening dark, I noticed that a fire was burning behind a rise in the ground several hundred yards away, and I concluded that the Fid'an were camping there.

Ali was still feeling too weak to walk with me, and I made my way alone to the fire. As I came near, I recognized the Fid'an sitting round the coffee-hearth.

"Dakhil! Protection!" I cried out.

One of the Bedouins sprang up, rifle in hand. He made

ready to fire, throwing the clip of cartridges into the breach and slamming the lever down. Involuntarily I shut my eyes and staggered, when I heard the voice of the *Akid* (leader) call out to the man not to shoot. The shock had been so great, however, that my knees gave way, and I toppled over. The *Akid,* who had saved my life, came to me. He had a small goat-skin bag filled with liquid butter in his hand, and made me take a few sips, and immediately I felt better.

He then led me to the fire and offered me coffee; and I knew by that token that my life was now under his protection.

I asked him for our clothing. He wanted to return it to me, but the other men grumbled and protested, and I had to be content with two old ragged herders' cloaks. I threw one over my shoulders and with the other and a skin of butter, went back to Ali, and after he had gulped down some of the butter, I supported him to the camp fire.

The Fid'an permitted us to seat ourselves among them, and Ali, too, was given coffee. It now turned out that our assailants were quite good fellows. Had we not started arguing when they fell upon us, we should have come off better. Now we were as safe among them as in Abraham's bosom.

In the course of our conversation that evening, I remembered the letter from Amir Fuaz to Hajem Pasha, the missive that had created such a lively disturbance in Aleppo.

"Dost thou read Arabic?" I asked the *Akid;* and when, as I expected, he replied, "No," I continued:

"Then dost thou at least know the signature of thy *sheykh* and the seal of Amir Fuaz?"

Before his men, the Fid'an dared not admit that this too was beyond him, so I asked for the pouch Ali used to carry on his body, containing the letter along with other treasures.

Everybody listened respectfully to Ali's reading of the letter. He read judiciously—only what was pleasant and polite; all the rest he left out. The rascals hung on Ali's lips and drank in every word that came from them. When he had finished reading and had kissed the signature and the seal, the men pressed round him and inspected with awe the astounding document; and ignorant as they were of writing, they looked at it upside down!

The *Akid* was visibly uneasy, and for a while he and the others put their heads together and, after much gesticulation and muttering, he turned to Ali and me and fired a cross-examination of silly questions at us. At last he seemed convinced that we had been wrongly treated, and he ordered his men to return our belongings to us. This naturally caused a small revolution, but the *Akid* knew how to make his influence felt, and after each of the men had in turn exhausted his protests against such a breach of the honour and the good customs of noble raiders, all our property was actually returned to us, with the exception only of my wrist watch, which still remained on the arm of the leader. Ali noticed it and, greatly daring, cried out: "Through thee the faith of thy *sheykh* is blackened! Divest thyself of our property, if thou art our friend." The *Akid* meekly handed over the watch, which Ali put on his own wrist. "Let me take care of it for thee," he said to me, in his protective manner. He is actually "taking care" of my watch to this very day!

Our Fid'an hosts numbered seventeen horsemen and eight camel-riders, who had come on the scene after the attack on us. A gang of typical desert outlaws.

At the evening meal they spread a large leather camel-saddle cover for a tablecloth. Previously the dough for our bread had been kneaded on it. At other times it served as manger and watering-trough for the horses and camels, for it could be suspended by leather loops, one at each of the four corners.

The *Akid* poured sour camels' milk from a goat skin into a wooden basin and handed it round. The few *dhaluls* were lying close to us. The red campfire threw a glow of light over them and their long shadows melted into the blackness of the night. For a moment I imagined myself surrounded by strange monsters.

When I closed my eyes and heard only the belching and grunting of my table-companions, I could scarcely distinguish them from the camels chewing the cud. And Ali was the noisiest feeder of them all!

Next morning the Fid'ans proposed that they should join us with the idea of entering Ruala territory and lifting some camels. Nothing remained for Ali and myself but to make the best of these unwelcome proposals. We had to endure their company in the pious hope that somewhere we should fall in with the Ruala Bedouins.

Two days later we camped at the well of Al-Hajal,

where our camels and horses were watered. One of the Fid'ans scraped a shallow hole in the soil and spread the saddle leather from one of the camels over it. Into this simple but practical trough we poured the stale water from the well.

After we had watered our animals, we travelled onward in the dry bed of the Al-Hajal *wadi*. We were crossing a flat between two branches of it when suddenly shots rang out and bullets whistled over our heads.

The Fid'an wheeled instantly to gallop out of range, but they did not get far. Our assailants, imperfectly visible but obviously numerous, followed up their warning volley with a raking fire that in as many seconds unhorsed four of the fugitives. Seeing that to escape was impossible, and to fight hopeless, they all stopped and signalled their surrender to the advancing force of camel-riders. More than a hundred of these had grown out of the ground, as it were, before my astonished eyes. The Fid'an had walked into a trap. They had been too reckless even to send scouts ahead.

I knew instantly that the newcomers were Ruala. The Saba have as intimate a knowledge of that region, but only the Ruala take the field with so many fine racing-camels; the Saba, like the Fid'an, favour horses.

"The Lord be with us!" exclaimed Matan, the leader of the Fid'an freebooters, now thoroughly frightened. He clearly thought himself lost; and he had every reason to believe that I should use the opportunity of paying him back in kind. But I reassured him. "We have made peace with thee," I said, "and I shall tell the leader of these Ruala that thou hast actually accorded us thy protection that we might safely reach the grazing grounds of our friends. I shall ask him to permit thee and thy men this evening to camp in peace with the Ruala."

"Truly, thou lightest up my countenance," the Fid'an replied, overjoyed, "and I swear that I have now restored everything." To my amazement, I saw in his extended hand my costly compass, which I had supposed lost.

The Ruala, swaying on the backs of lean *dhaluls,* were drawing nearer. Well ahead of them galloped a horseman on a "red" (bay) mare, obviously their leader, and I cantered to meet him. He had his *kaffiyah* drawn over his face, so that when we met I could see only his eyes, and his voice came muffled: "Who art thou, rider on the 'blue' (grey) mare?"

For answer, I uncovered my face and said: "I yield myself to thee. And all these men"—pointing to Ali and the Fid'an—"I put under thy protection, O *Akid,* in the name of my brother and thy Amir, Fuaz."

The Rueyli drove his heels into his mare so that she plunged wildly and he had great difficulty in controlling her. He pulled down his *kaffiyah* and I was greatly astonished to see that it was Fuaz himself, but beside himself with rage. "Ride away, my brother," he said, "lest thy blood be answerable for my deeds. Like the panther, I winded these dogs of Fid'an that dare to yelp in the grazing grounds of the Ruala."

He was berserk, mad with the fighting frenzy of the Sha'lan. He tossed off his cloak, which caught on his mare's croup; he bared his arms and chest; he shifted his carbine from hand to hand, while his horse curvetted under him. Argument was useless; I could do only one thing, appeal to his Bedouin sense of honour. "These men whom thou dost behold," I said, "have wholly refrained from shedding blood. And they have accompanied me in the confidence that thou wouldst grant them freedom and safety, for the sake of the friendship between thee and me."

The young *sheykh* had no word of reply for me, but his eyes spoke eloquently enough. They were full of hate and unbridled fury. Spasmodically he wheeled his poor mare in circles around me, himself driven by the pent-up storm within. I cried out to him at last to master his wrath and be his true self. Suddenly, he cantered back to his camel-riders, waiting some distance away. I felt with instinctive certainty that the fit of rage was over, and that my Fid'an wards were safe. In spite of all, I could not help admiring him. Fuaz might have said to me: "Forget, Aziz, that you intended to put these robbers under my protection." But I had uttered the word *dakhil* (protection in the sight of God) in my appeal. No human ears had heard it except Fuaz's and mine, yet God had heard; and that was binding on a Bedouin conscience—even that of a robber chief.

I assured the Fid'an that Amir Fuaz had taken them under his protection, and they had immediate confirmation of this when they saw the Ruala riders dismount and proceed to make camp. The Fid'an in their place followed suit. For reasons of ceremony, I remained with them for the time being. Presently Fuaz, accompanied by some of his men, strolled over and sat down by the Fid'an campfire. Nobody could have guessed from his manner that there had been any trouble. He was perfectly calm and thanked his enemies for their companionship and protection of me on my journey.

Only after coffee had made the rounds was there any mention of the Fid'an losses. The Ruala fire had cost them two mares and two *dhaluls*. Fuaz at once declared they should be recompensed by six of his best racing-camels. He was under no obligation to make any restitution; but the magnanimity of an Arab *sheykh* demands such acts of bounty.

When the two strangely assorted companies separated on the following morning, Fuaz took the precaution of attaching one of his body-slaves to the Fid'an. He was to see them to the first rise of the Abu Rijmeyn, well beyond the Ruala territory.

☙ XXVI ❧

The Stealing of the Mare

Aᴍɪʀ Fᴜᴀᴢ ʜᴀᴅ not brought his tribesmen to al-Hajal for the purpose of routing out marauding Fid'an. The encounter with them was accidental. The object of the Ruala *ghazu* (raid) was the recovery of a blood mare which the Saba had "lifted" a short time before. Falha, the "Luckbringer", as she was called, was of the best strain in Arabia and famed throughout the land. As soon as Fuaz learned that she had been taken, he dispatched Mnahi to the Saba with an offer of forty camels for her restitution—an exceedingly high value to put on a mare. But the Saba declined the offer. The only alternative to buying back Falha, as the Saba well knew, would be taking her back by force; and Fuaz honourably informed them that such was his intention. This did not amount to a declaration of war. It was rather a knightly challenge, and the rules of the game involved the tacit understanding that no blood should be shed unnecessarily on either side.

Fuaz's scouts—*Iyun*, the "eyes", the Bedouins call them—had tracked the mare to a Saba encampment in the vicinity and had thoroughly reconnoitered its surroundings. They had discovered that the Saba camels and horses, including Falha, were grazing under the guard of only a few youths, in a depression several miles away from the main camp, some seventy tents strong.

This disposition gave Fuaz twofold satisfaction. It would facilitate the execution of his plan to recover his mare by stratagem and confirmed his assumption that the Saba did not reckon with the possibility of a Ruala raid so soon, as very little rain had fallen in that region and travel therefore was still very difficult. They probably thought that the Ruala would not venture so far into the inner Hamad until much later, when water and pasture would be plentiful. It was clear at all events that, for the time being, Falha's keepers felt themselves quite secure. Furthermore, if a skirmish proved unavoidable, the fighting would be away from the Saba tents, for Bedouins of noble lineage consider it barbarous to engage the enemy near their own camp. They believe that only the Turks, the "Franks" (Europeans) and the rulers of agricultural Arabia wage war in such a way as to endanger the women and children.

Luck favoured Fuaz's designs from beginning to end. We broke camp early in the morning and a few hours later circled round the pasture where the Saba horses were. Then we wheeled and got between them and the camp. The whole movement was made smoothly and without contact with our opponents. But now their outposts sighted our troop and sought to evade us and carry word to the camp. Our camel-riders easily caught the fugitives, who stopped when a few shots were fired over their heads and let themselves be taken without attempting any defence. They were mere boys, fourteen to sixteen years of age. In rough jest, their captors cut off some of their long plaits and with these bound them hand and foot. This was a terrible indignity to such proud lads, who set great store by their six or eight "horns", as the Arabs call these tresses.

It was nearly midday when we reached the depression in which the horses were grazing. It was a lovely scene, the sky was blue, the brilliant spring sun warm and pleasant, and the air was filled with the sweet smell of the fresh herbage. The horses and camels ranged about, browsing quietly. The sleepy herders were totally unaware of our presence until our camel-riders suddenly appeared over the lip of the depression. Then they awoke to a realization of what was happening. I was rather loath to disturb their *dolce far niente;* above all was I sorry for the Saba horses, which were to be so suddenly driven from their delectable pasture.

The mares raised their heads inquisitively as the herders, rudely awakened from their siesta, sprang to their feet and yelled warnings one to the other. A few of them were successful in loosening the woollen shackles of their horses, and, leaping on their backs, made their escape. They were but a handful, however, and of these two or three were eventually captured.

The horses of the Saba became restive as the Ruala horsemen galloped about them, but, shackled by the forelegs, they could only hobble round helplessly.

At last our people cut out some twenty horses, including Falha, the brown mare of our search. Falha was shackled with iron links instead of the usual woollen ropes. Amir Fuaz had brought with him a couple of files in anticipation of such an eventuality. His delight on seeing Falha again was obvious; she was worth more to him and to the Ruala than all the rest of the horses put together. We now began in turns, two men at a time, to file through the iron shackles. When we had finished that task, Amir Fuaz kissed his mare's hoofs with joy.

Falha, feeling her freedom, commenced to prance and neigh while I held her by the halter. I begged Amir Fuaz to tie her to the saddle of my camel, so that I might lead her home. "Ride her!" he replied, and explained that we must mount the captured horses in order to get as far away from the enemy as possible in the shortest space of time. So I jumped on Falha's back and galloped off with my friends to where the camel-riders with the prisoners were awaiting us.

In all, the Ruala had seized twenty-three mares. As we bade farewell to the Saba herders, one of them, a young lad, stepped up to Amir Fuaz and cried:

"*Ayb*"—"Shame on thee!"

"Who art thou?" asked the young Prince.

"Jaza ibn Ajlan."

"And what is thy desire?"

"Behold—only with tears can I water Freyha (the Joybringer) when thou takest her away, and she will not again have the milk of her Naga (Milch-camel), and Simiha (the Soft-one) and Nauma (the Sleepy-one) and her daughters will also mourn for her."

Amir Fuaz appreciated the lad's grief for his lost mares and asked him further:

"And how old are Simiha and Nauma?" .

"Simiha is one summer old and Nauma two. But see, Freyha is again in foal!"

"And therefore thou would'st have back the mother of thy foals?"

"Not because of that, but because it is a shame that thou shouldst steal the *wool*-shackled mares from our pastures."

"Did I not honourably warn you?"

"We trusted thy word, which only referred to Falha, and therefore we shackled her with *steel*; all the other mares had only *woollen* shackles."

Amir Fuaz looked thoughtfully into the distance and, as was his habit, toyed with his hair-plaits. Then, twisting one of the locks round his index finger, he stared the young Saba straight in the eyes.

"Thou art daring. But thou speakest the truth and I am not offended. Now I understand why Falha alone wore iron shackles. Therefore I will reward thy trust. Falha is our booty; take back what belongs to thee."

The Prince ordered his men to dismount from the captured mares and return them to the Saba. He also commanded Mnahi to take the plaits cut from the heads of the young Saba from his saddlebag, into which he had stuffed them as souvenirs, and throw them away.

As Fuaz noticed me sitting peacefully and satisfied on Falha, he burst out laughing and cried:

"Allah Karim!—God is benevolent! Look at Aziz. First he comes on a raid against us, then we capture him, and now he rides home on our best mare."

Ali, my gallant protector, who stood near, took up the joke:

"Amir Fuaz will permit me to say that one must

watch Aziz carefully, or he may flee to your enemies with Falha."

"Allah give him strength," said Fuaz. "He rides with the panthers and the falcons!"

"With the lions!" was Ali's improvement.

Despite their show of cheerfulness, I could see that it went hard with the Ruala tribesmen to watch the Saba ride off with the captured mares. But no one uttered a word of complaint against the magnanimous gesture of the chief, for generosity is held to be the highest virtue amongst the Bedouins.

So we started on our long ride to the home camp, and eleven days later rested again under the hospitable roof of Nuri Sha'lan's dwelling.

⚙ XXVII ⚙

Anaga—the Falcon

THE FALCONER'S SONG

Arise, my brother!
Let us away to hunt with the hungry *silek;* [1]
Set the daring falcon upon my gauntleted fist,
Bring the leashed hounds,
And saddle my finely built *dhalul.*
Tie my speediest horse to her girth—
The mare of noble birth.
Let us ride once more
With the daughters of our blood,
With the wandering herds and our tribe
And the leader of our people.
Beloved friends!
To-day we ride with jubilant song,
Into the welcoming wilderness,
The hounds accompanying us in joyous voice,
And the mare with whinnying calls;
Never shall I tire of watching
The wonderful flight of the proud falcon
As he breasts the wind,
And how his golden eyes hold
The prey which his strong talons shall seize.

The advance guard of the migrating Ruala had already reached the neighbourhood of the rain pools of Khabra Mirfiah, whence every day messengers brought word of new thunderstorms. In that region we could

[1] Singular. *Sluki.* Greyhound.

therefore expect to find game in great numbers, and Amir Fuaz had immediate preparations made for a great hunt with his falcons and greyhounds.

For two days prior to the hunt, falcons and Sulkan were given nothing to eat. The slender hounds, lying about half-starved between the legs of the camels, seemed skinnier than usual, and the hungry falcons complained, crooning loudly and anxiously when anyone passed near them. The slaves had hooded them now, with small helmets of red, blue, black or green. These pretty leather hoods were ornamented with gold and silver thread.

On the appointed morning, when the hunt had assembled, Amir Fuaz mounted his war-mare. Dugan, one of his slaves, unhooded his pet falcon. Fuaz, about sixty paces away, gave the falconer's cry, and the bird straightened, recognizing its master's voice. Dugan let go the jess which he had held in his gauntleted hand, and instantly the bird rose, and, flying like an arrow to the Prince, settled on his raised right arm. Fuaz drew a hood over the falcon's eyes again.

"This is Anaga, the 'Meteor'," he said to me. "He drops from the upper sky and slays his opponent in the plunge. He can sail the higher heavens as safely as he can skim over the surface of the earth. To-day thou wilt see what Anaga can do."

At a sign from Amid Fuaz, we set out. The "whips" called their slim greyhounds by name: Shillah, Satha, Tarfa, and so forth.

They were unleashed only when the last tents were left behind and there was no more danger of the large wolflike watchdogs and herd-dogs attacking the more delicate hounds and tearing them to pieces.

Twelve of the Amir's slaves carried hunting-hawks, each bird hooded and in full attire. Relatives of the Prince and other Ruala nobles also carried falcons on their mares, some of the birds borne on the riders' gauntleted wrists, others, in fact the majority, on the sheep skin which is spread over the horse's croup, when the Bedouin goes hunting.

The "*Sala*" or beater corps, comprising more than three hundred camel-riders and about two hundred horsemen, began to spread out right and left, to round up and drive the game towards the centre of our line. Ringed by the greyhounds, our wild troop galloped over the wide plain in the fresh morning air. Our hearts beat with excitement. It was to be an auspicious and lucky day, according to every soothsayer whom Fuaz had consulted during the past days.

The young Prince galloped at my side. On his raised fist sat Anaga, in its red leather hood embroidered with gold thread, on the top of which was sewn a beautiful pearl; and instead of eyes there blazed on its sides two precious emeralds.

"Aziz," cried Fuaz to me, "I love the wine of war— but, oh! I also like to drink the milk of the chase. Is not hunting the sister of war and the quarry a warrior struck to earth?"

He reined in, and I also pulled up my mare, to let the train of hunting comrades ride past. They were a splendid knightly troop, on beautiful mares and camels. The falcons balanced with outstretched wings on the wrists of riders and the croups of the galloping horses. Cloaks, manes, and tails, plaits and head-cloths, saddle trappings, fringes, and tassels flapped in the wind. The shout of men mingled with the thunder of hoofs, the neighing of the mares, the screams of the hawks and the baying of the hounds.

Knee to knee, I galloped on with Amir Fuaz. Sharp eyes descried a heron rising higher and higher into the blue, although herons are rarely seen in this part of Arabia. Probably this one was on its way to the marsh-lands of Southern Mesopotamia. The young Amir was all excitement; he uttered piercing yells and cried rapturously:

"O my eye, my snatcher, there is thy prey!" and with trembling fingers, still galloping, he attempted to remove the hood and leg-strap of the falcon.

"O thou flash of lightning! O thou sword of the sky!"

The Prince was particularly devoted to this falcon. It was a tercel through its fifth moult, and a present from Ibn Khalifa, the Sheykh of Bahrein, who had procured it from the Bedouins of Jabal Shammar in exchange for a valuable mare. Having taken off hood and leg-strap, Fuaz swung Anaga up and down on his fist and then sideways.

"Open thy swift wings!" he cried.

With easy beat of wings and whining cries, the splendid bird rose into the air. Instinctively we drew rein to watch the spectacle. At first the falcon beat upward, but after a while he stooped and sailed in long flight close above the ground, without seeming to pay any attention to the heron.

One could only suppose that the bird took pleasure in the sweep of its flight and its skimming and turning close to the ground. Then, with a bold, effortless swing, Anaga rose in wide spirals higher and higher into the sky.

With short, vigorous wing-beats he flew above and beyond the heron. Suddenly Anaga turned, and with folded wings swooped upon the larger bird, but with a swift swerve the falcon shot past and utilised the speed of his downward plunge for another upward curve, which brought him into the eye of the wind and to a higher and more advantageous position. There he circled, watching for a while; then hovered in one spot motionless, like a star in the heavens.

Fuaz, watching his pet, called out joyfully:

"Now shalt thou see the heron falling into his claws as a fish into the fisherman's net!"

Still Anaga hung on motionless wings. Was he choosing the best course for his fateful plunge? Suddenly he gave one beat of the wings and stooped, wings folded, legs pressed close to the body, hurtling down like a projectile. Yet the big heron saw the lunge in time to measure its pace and escape on rapidly beating wings. Instantly the hawk checked his plunge; with an almost imperceptible movement of the wings, he changed direction, and at once was in full cry after the heron.

Now he lowered the path of his flight somewhat, closer to the heron; and now he swooped right over him, only his breast feathers touching, but the terrible gripping talon shot out and held the great bird by the neck. Tumbling over and over, the locked combatants came dashing earthwards. Torn feathers were scattered in the air. In the headlong tumble the falcon managed always to keep on top, and finally to release himself from the dangerous wings of the heron and give him the death-stroke with his knifelike claws. Only an experienced falcon can so release itself at the right moment.

The clever falcon was already soaring again when the body of his victim hit the ground with a dull thud. Anaga whirled aloft as straight as a fountain, only to return to us in an elegant curve. The wind whistled through its feathers as it swooped past our heads. In rapture, Amir Fuaz cried to his hawk:

"Anaga, O thou Meteor, O snatcher, O my eye!"

The blood-splashed, broad-shouldered falcon cooed happily, as if he understood the compliment, and with outstretched talons and widespread pinions, alighted gently on the raised fist of his master, who tenderly stroked the dishevelled feathers. As if drunk with blood, the bird began to shake himself, fluffed his plumage and smoothed it again, and blinked his gold-rimmed black eyes with their grey lids. Anaga was a diabolical creature, truly a bandit, but without doubt the crown of falconry amongst the Ruala was his by right.

For his magnificent aerial combat the slaves rewarded Anaga with a live pintail grouse which someone had caught. The falcon killed it by ripping its throat, tore out one wing, which he devoured, in order to reach lungs and heart. Then he tore and ate the strongest muscles of the breast. All else he left untouched.

A horseman galloped towards two greyhounds dragging up the dead heron, and took the bird from them.

The handsome crown feathers he plucked and presented to Amir Fuaz.

Our beaters meanwhile had been starting hares and other small game. The falcons used for such small fry were not of the same noble class as Anaga. The seemingly helpless hares had a means of defence, dangerous to their attackers, in the earth, which they can hug so closely and on which they can twist and double so quickly. One of the falcons injured its wings so badly that it could no longer fly. But in spite of all, most of the hawks were clever enough to make their kills by driving their talons between the hares' ribs into their lungs. After a kill, the huntsmen had to hurry and throw a cloak over the falcon to prevent its feeding on its quarry before the hare's throat was slit. This prescribed method of slaughtering is not peculiar to the Jews only, but to the Ishmaelites also, for meat from which the blood has not been drained is forbidden as human food.

The greyhounds were also set on the hares, but always in pairs. One dog gave chase, while the other cut off the hares' flight in another direction. But to catch the hare was no easy task, and many a greyhound took a somersault when a hare doubled suddenly.

❦ XXVIII ❦

The Young Gazelle Buck

A FALCON SUDDENLY LEFT his riding-perch amidst the advancing hunt and flew back. The huntsmen called to him threateningly, but in vain. Like an arrow he darted so close past the neck of my horse that automatically I leaned out of the saddle to avoid being struck. He turned in a flash and landed not far from me. I reined in and watched. With his out-spread tail propped on the ground, the falcon was grappling a snake in his talons, and with his beak striking at its elusive head. The snake writhed and coiled round the bird spasmodically, but could get no purchase on the plumage. At last, the falcon seized the viper's head and with a few circular movements twisted it off. A number of other huntsmen had stopped to watch the snake-killer at work, but when the struggle was over, and the bird started to eat its kill, one of them cried commandingly:

"Suhayl!"

Obediently the hawk left his quarry, and flew toward the upheld fist of the falconer, but just as he seemed about to settle on it, he suddenly veered, shot upward, and swept away like a stone hurled from a catapult. For a moment he hovered, high in the sky, then passed from our sight forever.

"The devil!" cried someone, and laughed.

"He is truly a devil!" remarked Amir Fuaz. "Few

falcons have such sight and still fewer such spirit. It is well that he seeks a mate. God grant that one day we may find his brood."

The call of the wild had lured Suhayl away, and he had obeyed the impulse of his blood.

With loud cries the Bedouins urged their mares forward, again racing each other. For today, however, though it was still early, the chase was over; for the heat of the sun is considered harmful to both greyhounds and falcons.

Amir Fuaz gave the order to rally, and we all proceeded to the previously appointed camping-place, where shortly after the pack-camels arrived with waterskins. In a straight line we were, at the most, seven miles from the main Ruala camp, but in our criss-cross riding we had covered nearly thrice that distance.

When fuel had been collected, coffee was made and hares and bustards roasted. From all quarters riders came in on breathless horses. Groups of men clustered round the small fires. The camel-riders of our beater-corps trickled in, bringing an abundance of game—pintail grouse, bustards, hares, foxes, badgers, gazelles. All the carcasses were ranged on the ground near Amir Fuaz and the other *shiyukhs*.

The thirsty mares were watered only after they had rested awhile, but the panting and tired greyhounds had water splashed into their mouths immediately. The falconers placed their hawks in cooking-vessels, partly filled with water, wherein the dusty birds fluffed and preened their feathers.

Huntsmen lay at ease, sipping coffee and talking.

Near me a fine, full-grown, reddish-brown falcon sat captive on a horizontal perch. It fluttered its wings and tried to fly away, but a strong leather strap held it fast. It had been captured only two days before, and its eyelids were still sewn together, as is the Bedouin practice with newly caught hawks. Dugan, the hawking-slave, had brought this wild bird along to accustom it to the riding.

Towards evening, Fuaz sent some horsemen to the tribal encampment (the Ruala were in migration), to ascertain where his tent was pitched, and after supper, under the shining moon, we all set out for it.

That moonlight ride through the tranquil night was a wonderful experience. Widely spread out, in smaller or larger groups, we rode along at a walk. Mnahi, chief of the Amir's bodyguard, beat time to the Bedouin songs, which from a distance sounded like a faint, "Yo-ho-loo-oo, Yo-ho-loo-oo."

Riding up a rise, I could fancy that the earth ended beyond it; I always expected to find a dark abyss with an illuminated ocean, opal light and stars rising from its depths.

Lights did in fact appear as we topped one ridge—red campfires. They covered the plain below far and wide. It was a great Ruala encampment that lay before us in the shimmering moonlight—a magic picture, a fairy-tale of the desert. Distant murmurs fell on our ears, bringing a touch of reality to the unreal.

We rode down, a wave of singing horsemen, that melted away into the shadows of the black tents. Here we dismounted, tied our horses to the tent ropes, and entered the goat-hair roofs to sit round the camel-dung fires.

After midnight the parties broke up and we returned to our own camping-place. The Bedouins love these nocturnal palavers and, when not wandering, rest during the day in preparation for the long evening sittings.

We rolled up in our sheep skins for some hours, close to the fire, for the night had turned bitterly cold. Scarcely had we fallen asleep when it seemed to be time to get up again. It was still dark. Muffled figures rose and moved to the glowing embers, warmed their hands over them and thrust twigs into them to light their cigarettes.

"Get up, children!" was the cry.

The slaves went down the lines of camels, took off their woollen knee-hobbles and kicked or slapped them on the flanks. One by one the *dhaluls*, shadowy in the dark, rose and were saddled. The mares were as yet spared; they were to be ridden only in the chase. We led them with us, as usual, tied to our camels.

Dawn passed into a glowing, golden morning. Far out over the plain everything appeared pure and transparent, even in the farthest distance. Our spirits were refreshed, our senses awakened. The hunters changed from camel to horseback when we neared the ponds of Khabra Mirfiah, toward which ran many gazelle tracks.

Our beaters swarmed out and quickly put up a troop of gazelles, which they drove toward us.

The wild hunt was up. Halloo! How our mares stretched out! How the hoofs flew, as hunters and hunted spread out over the plain and the drivers put up ever new herds before them!

A group of riders, of which I was one, came almost within striking distance of one band, but the fleet gazelles always managed to elude us. The headlong ride had already lasted more than an hour, and our horses trembled and panted from exhaustion. Some gazelles had succeeded in breaking through the scattered line of hunters.

Amir Fuaz and his men now unhooded and released their falcons. The liberated birds shot away. With incredible speed they overtook the gazelles and chose their victims. At first they flew above them close to the ground, then swept forward and obtained a hold between their horns or on their necks. With desperate plunges and side springs the terrified gazelles endeavoured to free themselves from their murderous assailants, but without avail. With their talons hooked in the scalp or the eye-sockets of the gazelles, the falcons struck wildly with their wings and beaks at their eyes to impede their progress.

Horrified, I reined in my mare. A blinded gazelle dashed past me, but she was no longer able to escape the pack of greyhounds which, overtaking her, seized her hocks which they did not release even when they tumbled over and over. From the swirling cloud of dust came the bleating, bellowing, and groaning of the stricken gazelle, which ceased only when the huntsmen, racing up, put an end to the animal's suffering.

The falcons soared above the heads of men and beasts, all wild with the excitement and the lust of killing. The beautiful defenceless gazelles lay quivering on the sand.

Five gazelles fell victims to the falcons and grey-hounds at the first charge, and thirty-one more before the huntsmen decided they had had enough and turned homeward.

The gamest fight I have ever seen was put up by a young gazelle buck. He had succeeded in shaking off two falcons and goring a greyhound, and had reached temporary safety. We could still see him quite clearly, but a long way off, standing on the watch, waiting. Our extended line of mounted beaters converged to hem him in, and the hunt of the poor buck started afresh. In my heart, I prayed that the gallant fellow might escape for good, but it looked as if he were spent. Our horsemen drew nearer and nearer and, when the ring had reached striking distance, three strong hawks flew at the buck. In no time they were upon him; and once more we beheld a desperate contest.

The Ruala had agreed that this fight was to be fought out by the falcons alone, without help from the grey-hounds.

Our troop of horsemen galloped, shouting, after the fleeing buck. He was not a hundred horse-lengths ahead, so that we could clearly follow his contest with the three falcons, and we came steadily nearer. Suddenly he would swerve away, throw himself on the ground, turn somer-saults and speed on again, doubling right and left. It was no easy task for the falcons to get the better of this master of the art of defence.

It was probably not his first fight against the terrible hunting-hawks.

These hawks, too, were masters in their way. Despite the buck's resourcefulness, two of them managed at last to fasten on his head and neck. Suddenly riotous shouts of applause from the huntsmen rose above the panting of the horses and the drumming of their hoofs. But these plaudits were not for the falcons; they were for the doughty buck. He had checked abruptly in mid-career and leaped bolt upright in the air. With the same mighty swing he threw himself on the ground, tumbled over, and with a sidelong thrust of the head, drove his small dirklike horns into the ground, and executed a few more somersaults, having maimed one hawk, gored another to death, and crushed the third, which had fastened upon him but a few moments before.

It looked as if the buck could never rise again, that all his delicate bones must be broken.

The whole episode had taken place with the speed of lightning—and there was the desperate animal on his legs again, and off in full flight once more, before one had time to take in what had happened.

Fearing that the buck would be lost, the huntsmen unleashed the greyhounds after all; but it was too late. The hounds chased for some time after the little cloud of dust far ahead of them, but the hero of the day disappeared in the glassy distance.

"*Ya ishli—ya ishli!*" the huntsmen shouted—the rallying cry of the Bedouin to his hounds.

Our ride back was not like our merry ride out in the morning. Many of our mares were lame, yet they had to carry not only their tired masters, but the best part of the hunting trophies; and several injured greyhounds into the bargain.

Noticing on Amir Fuaz's *aba* droppings of his falcon, I attempted to brush it off, but the young Prince stopped me and said proudly: "No—no, Aziz! The excrement of the noble falcons stamps us with the hall-mark of noble birth."

His words explained better than any conception of mine the true inwardness of these hunts; they are considered noble and honourable. The nobility of the desert (its "large-eyedness" as the Bedouins call it) must be experienced and tested; but noble and large-eyed as the Bedouins are, so are also their horses, camels, greyhounds, and falcons, and no less the Bedouin's prey—gazelles, antelopes, and ostriches.

But the ignoble man or beast the wandering Arab despises. He holds them beyond the pale, beyond the law of the desert . . .

> ". . . die that they might have new life;
> For only what is weakling dies,
> That what is strong may live."

Other Hungry Mind Finds
available from
Hungry Mind Press:

A Book of One's Own
by Thomas Mallon
ISBN: 1-886913-02-1

Days and Nights in Calcutta
by Clark Blaise and Bharati Mukherjee
ISBN: 1-886913-01-3

Passage to Ararat
by Michael Arlen
ISBN: 1-886913-05-6

The Tree Farm
by Robert Treuer
ISBN: 1-886913-06-4

The Soul of the Night
by Chet Raymo
ISBN: 1-886913-11-0

Honey From Stone
by Chet Raymo
ISBN: 1-886913-12-9

A False Spring
by Pat Jordan
ISBN: 1-886913-22-6

Laughing in the Hills
by Bill Barich
ISBN: 1-886913-20-X